AN EXHIBITION OF SCROLLS
AND ARCHEOLOGICAL ARTIFACTS
FROM THE COLLECTIONS OF THE
ISRAEL ANTIQUITIES AUTHORITY

AYALA SUSSMANN AND RUTH PELED

LIBRARY OF CONGRESS·WASHINGTON
IN ASSOCIATION WITH
THE ISRAEL ANTIQUITIES AUTHORITY

SCROLLS
FROM THE
DEAD SEA

GEORGE BRAZILLER · NEW YORK

Published in 1993 by George Braziller, Inc., by arrangement with the Library of Congress

Printed in the United States of America
97 96 95 94 93   1 2 3 4 5

For information, please address the publisher:
George Braziller, Inc.
60 Madison Avenue
New York, New York 10010

LIBRARY OF CONGRESS CATALOGING-IN-PUBLICATION DATA

Scrolls from the Dead Sea : an exhibition of scrolls and archeological artifacts from the collections of the Israel Antiquities Authority / [edited by] Ayala Sussmann and Ruth Peled.
    p.   cm.
    Catalog issued in conjunction with an exhibition held at the Library of Congress, Apr. 29–Aug. 1, 1993; the New York Public Library, Oct. 2, 1993–Jan. 8, 1994; the M. H. de Young Memorial Museum, Feb. 26–May 8, 1994.
    Includes facsimiles of selected texts with English translation.
    Includes bibliographical references and index.
    ISBN 0-8076-1333-9
    1. Dead Sea scrolls — Exhibitions. 2. Manuscripts, Hebrew — Jerusalem — Exhibitions. 3. Qumran site — Exhibitions. 4. Qumran community — Exhibitions. 5. Israel. Rashut ha-'atiḳot — Library — Exhibitions. I. Sussmann, Ayala. II. Peled, Ruth. III. Israel. Rashut ha-'atiḳot. IV. Library of Congress. V. New York Public Library. VI. M. H. de Young Memorial Museum. VII. Dead Sea scrolls. English & Hebrew. Selections. 1993.
BM487.S37 1993
296.1'55'07473 — dc20

92-20476

CIP

This publication meets the minimum requirements of American National Standard for Information Sciences—Permanence of Paper for Printed Library Materials. ANSI Z39.48–1984.

Produced for publication by
ARCHETYPE PRESS, INC., Washington, D.C.
Diane Maddex, Project Director
Robert L. Wiser, Art Director
Gretchen Smith Mui, Editorial Assistant

Jacket and opening pages: Detail from the Psalms Scroll (catalog no. 5; see pages 52–55). Copied ca. 30–50 C.E., this impressive scroll is a liturgical collection of psalms and hymns, comprising parts of biblical as well as noncanonical psalms.

CONTENTS

FOREWORD

James H. Billington
Librarian
of Congress

Scrolls from the Dead Sea, the exhibition described in this catalog, includes twelve fragmentary scrolls as well as a selection of archeological artifacts excavated at the Qumran ruin in the Judean Desert. These scrolls and artifacts also form the nucleus of two related exhibitions, the first at the New York Public Library and the second at the M. H. de Young Memorial Museum in San Francisco. The Library of Congress is publishing this catalog on behalf of all the venues, in association with the Israel Antiquities Authority.

The Israel Antiquities Authority approached the Library of Congress in December 1991 with an extraordinary proposal: to organize an exhibition of selected Dead Sea Scrolls from its collections in Jerusalem. I communicated our keen interest immediately. After all, from the moment of their discovery in 1947, these manuscripts have ignited the imagination of specialists and non-specialists alike. Hidden for almost two thousand years in remote caves, the Dead Sea Scrolls are regarded by many as the greatest manuscript find of the twentieth century.

At the Library of Congress we have augmented the items borrowed from the Israel Antiquities Authority with materials from our own Hebraic, rare book, manuscript, motion picture, print, map, and photographic collections. We describe these supplementary materials in a separate interpretive brochure.

This catalog uses the scrolls, artifacts, and supplementary materials to relate the story of the scrolls' discovery and to provide their historical and archeological context. We introduce the texts with transcriptions, translations, and explanations; explore the various theories concerning the nature of the Qumran community, its identity, and its theology; and discuss the challenges facing modern researchers as they struggle to reconstruct the texts and contexts from the thousands of fragments that remain. The exhibition enables visitors to understand the nature and working methods of archeologists, historians, linguists, and paleographers.

It is especially fitting that this historic exhibition is opening at the Library of Congress, because the first time the Dead Sea Scrolls were exhibited in the United States was in October 1949, in the Great Hall of the Library's Thomas Jefferson Building. The three Dead Sea Scrolls then displayed belonged to Mar Athanasius Yeshua Samuel, Metropolitan of the Syrian Jacobite Monastery of St. Mark in Jerusalem, who purchased them from a Bethlehem antiquities dealer and then brought them to the United States in early 1949. These scrolls were sold by the Metropolitan in 1954 and are currently on display in Israel's Shrine of the Book, the Jerusalem museum that was dedicated to the discoveries in the Judean Desert.

This exhibition reflects the Library's abiding interest in mounting exhibitions that present and interpret the written legacy of world civilizations. Other such exhibitions include Living Traditions of Russian Faith: Books and Manuscripts of the Old Believers (May 31 to June 29, 1990), From the Ends of the Earth: Judaic Treasures of the Library of Congress (June 19 to September 8, 1991), and Rome Reborn: The Vatican Library and Renaissance Culture (January 8 to April 30, 1993). From the Ends of the Earth, which marked the seventy-fifth anniversary of the establishment of the Hebraic collections of the Library of Congress, documented the national library's long-standing commitment to collect, preserve, and make available materials relating to the spiritual and cultural heritage of the Jewish people.

Scores of talented individuals, working in Jerusalem, New York, San Francisco, and Washington, have collaborated to make this complex undertaking possible. At the Library of Congress the project team included Norma Baker, director of development; Irene Burnham, director of interpretive programs; Michael W. Grunberger, head of the Hebraic Section; Doris A. Hamburg, acting conservation officer; and Tambra Johnson, registrar.

Once again it is my pleasant duty to thank the Project Judaica Foundation and especially its president, Mark E. Talisman, who continues to provide steadfast and generous support for the Judaic program at the national library. The foundation's support for this project from its inception has made possible this exhibition and its catalog.

This complex international traveling exhibition carried with it extensive security, preservation, courier, and shipping requirements. We are deeply grateful for the indemnification provided by the Federal Council on the Arts and the Humanities for the scrolls and artifacts borrowed from the Israel Antiquities Authority. We are thankful, as well, for the logistical support and creative solutions provided by Delta Air Lines, the official airline of this exhibition. Additional support has come from Hilton International.

I am pleased that our efforts at the Library of Congress will permit these scrolls and artifacts to be seen by hundreds of thousands of visitors at the exhibition's respective venues in Washington, New York, and San Francisco. This exhibition is the result of rewarding cooperation between the Library of Congress and its partners, the Israel Antiquities Authority, the New York Public Library, and the Fine Arts Museums of San Francisco. We are especially grateful to Gen. Amir Drori, the director of the Israel Antiquities Authority, under whose leadership this exhibition was conceived and executed. Reflected throughout the exhibition and catalog are the skills and expertise of the Israel Antiquities Authority's talented staff of curators and conservators.

This catalog includes a preface by my late friend and colleague Father Timothy Healy, president of the New York Public Library. Written not long before he died on December 30, 1992, the preface captures his unique combination of faith, humor, and scholarship. He was a great leader of a great library, and he will be sorely missed by friends of libraries and learning the world over.

ISRAEL ANTIQUITIES AUTHORITY

Amir Drori
Director

This publication celebrates a happy event: the opportunity has finally presented itself for the Israel Antiquities Authority to exhibit a representative selection of original manuscripts of the Dead Sea Scrolls, together with related artifacts from the excavations at the Qumran site. The story of the discovery of these fascinating two thousand-year-old manuscripts has been related before: how the first cache of scrolls was revealed in 1947, how they were then purchased, and how excavations conducted in the area yielded further scrolls.

The difficulties in presenting the scrolls to the public, however, have frequently been distorted. It has always been our intent to unravel the meaning of these intriguing manuscripts and to present the findings to the public in a balanced and just manner. Scholars have been toiling at this task since the early days after the discovery. Hundreds of volumes have been published on the scrolls, and many more are expected. Nevertheless, it may be years before the true meaning and implications of these texts are fully comprehended. Our paramount concern has long been that the texts themselves be more widely viewed without endangering the state of their preservation.

It is toward this end that a carefully arranged showing of selected biblical and sectarian scrolls seemed a fitting endeavor. The timing of this exhibition appears to coincide with the demand of an increasingly wide and curious public for more information on the Dead Sea Scrolls. Much ink has been spilled on their "mystery." Texts that unfold not only the occurrences of two thousand years ago but also deeply rooted convictions are indeed mystifying. But these texts are not secret, and it is with pleasure that we, as keepers of the scrolls, are able to share a sampling with interested lay persons and scholars.

The splendid premises of the Library of Congress, the New York Public Library, and the M. H. de Young Memorial Museum are beyond doubt worthy stages for the display of this cherished collection of manuscripts—a cultural legacy common to the major monotheistic religions. The present exhibition is a product of fruitful collaboration among the Library of Congress, the New York Public Library, and the Israel Antiquities Authority. The initiative of Librarian of Congress James H. Billington, the president of the New York Public Library, Timothy Healy, and the enthusiastic cooperation of their staffs encouraged our own staff in its efforts to prepare this project. We are grateful to them all.

Our warm gratitude and appreciation are extended to Shelby White, Leon Levy, Estanne Abraham-Fawer, and Cyril Stein for their generosity and support of this and other projects of the Israel Antiquities Authority. Special thanks are due the Wolfson Family Charitable Trust for its generous contribution toward the Dead Sea Scrolls preservation project and to the Israel Ministry of Foreign Affairs and Shmuel Hadas for their continuous support.

In December 1991 Gen. Amir Drori, director of the Israel Antiquities Authority, visited the New York Public Library and raised with us the possibility of an exhibition based on the Dead Sea Scrolls. It was clear immediately that it would not be enough merely to show the scrolls, pinned on the wall as objects of veneration. Any exhibition worthy of the name would have to set them in a living context, bring them back to the life they once had for those who wrote them, and show their relevance for us two thousand years later.

Because the New York Public Library believed that it had the resources to do this, we agreed to cooperate with the Israel Antiquities Authority and the Library of Congress to develop an exhibition of the scrolls and supplement it with artifacts on loan from Israel that were found near the scrolls and are known to be contemporary with them. For the presentation in New York, these materials would be enhanced by books, maps, and manuscript materials from the library's own collections.

At the time of General Drori's visit, the Dead Sea Scrolls were much in the daily press. Scholar after scholar, mounted in full battle array, poured forth scorn and contumely on every other scholar brave enough to wander the Dead Sea landscape. In no sense did the New York Public Library wish to involve itself or its people in the give-and-take of the learned vendettas that make the academic world such an endearingly nasty place in which to live and work. Any research library as inclusive as this one has a catholicity of view that renders it immune to the ebb and flow of even the most learned venom.

The oldest scrolls appear to go as far back as the third century B.C.E., with the very real possibility, as Robert Alter points out in *Commentary,* that some of the texts are echoes of much earlier documents. They were written for and by a religious commune situated outside Jerusalem. That commune was the forerunner of at least some contemporary religious groups in that it appears to have lived in total isolation, with heavy apocalyptic expectations. Alter says, "They withdrew from the teeming city to a rock-strewn desert, hearkening to the voice of their master and awaiting the destruction of their enemies."

The scrolls contain fragments of all the books of the Hebrew Bible (with the exception of Esther) as well as a complete text of Isaiah. Such manuscripts are important for those who labor at the history of the Bible, but, as Alter points out, the fragments of the Apocrypha are more illuminating because we have known them so far only in Greek or Latin. Now, for the first time, the scrolls give us Hebrew or Aramaic originals of works we previously could read only in translation.

The scrolls are clearly the works of a small sect, convinced that it was continuing the great age of the composition of the Bible (historical distance notwithstanding) and essentially withdrawn from the vibrant, concomitant beginnings of both Rabbinical Judaism and Christianity. Alter comments that such an orientation toward history joined to a removal from the give-and-take of daily life encourages "megalomaniac self-importance and a contempt

NEW YORK
PUBLIC
LIBRARY

Timothy S. Healy
President

9

for others as well as a kind of hallucinatory relation to present events." We would be hard put to find a more adequate general comment on the scholarly brawl that has erupted over the past three years.

At the same time, their cloistered nature is one aspect of the scrolls that suits a research library. The community from which they came was the keeper of a live and very great tradition, no matter what use they intended at a given moment to make of it. In that sense Qumran was a place of quiet, of research, of withdrawal and reflection. Seen by themselves the scrolls are dark, mysterious, and, except by an expert, indecipherable. The same is profoundly true of research in most subjects, as well as of the places that house the materials for research. All of us at the New York Public Library thought that it was appropriate for this house of learning to exhibit works that came from a contemplative community striving both to understand and to escape the rigors of living under an imposed cosmopolitanism, in a time of strife, when it was all too easy to imagine the ending of worlds.

In a far more local sense, this exhibition also tells us about the Jewish Division of the New York Public Library. That division was established in 1897, only two years after the founding of the library itself and well before the opening of the great building on 42nd Street and Fifth Avenue. Since those early days it has been a valuable research and reference tool for a hugely varied public. It was the workshop for those who compiled the *Jewish Encyclopedia* at the beginning of the century, and it was where Eliezer Ben Yehuda, the father of modern Hebrew, labored during World War I on his monumental *Complete Dictionary of Ancient and Modern Hebrew.*

In tribute to this service, once the library had restored the D. Samuel and Jeane H. Gottesman Exhibition Hall in 1984, within a few years it brought before the public a sampling of its riches in Judaica. That exhibition, A Sign and a Witness: 2,000 Years of Hebrew Books and Illuminated Manuscripts, drew attention in America and abroad to the New York Public Library as a major resource for Jewish studies. The exhibition itself consisted of a dazzling array of Hebrew manuscripts, including the Dead Sea Scroll known as the Nahum Commentary and a collection of illuminated medieval manuscripts drawn from Europe, America, and Israel. About half of the 180 items in this memorable exhibition were from the library's own holdings.

The library is pleased and proud to present this new exhibition of the scrolls themselves. Peering through them into a past that we know only through fragments of fact and mountains of conjecture is a humbling experience. Few of the thousands who will look at them will be able to decipher their script, but everyone who stands before them will feel close to men and women caught in a time of strife, trouble, fright, and hope two thousand years ago. At least in these dimensions, they speak prophetically to our own days.

We offer thanks to Gen. Amir Drori and his staff at the Israel Antiquities Authority for being the "onlie begetter" of the exhibition itself and for their constant help, good will, thoughtfulness, and generosity through the process of putting it together. We also extend thanks to our esteemed colleague James H. Billington and his staff at the Library of Congress for sharing with us the joy of planning and realizing the complicated but fascinating exhibitions at our libraries.

The New York Public Library congratulates Susan F. Saidenberg, the manager of exhibitions, and her dedicated staff. Thanks also are due Leonard S. Gold, the Dorot chief librarian of the library's Jewish Division, who is our curator of this exhibition.

Finally, to everyone who will see for the first time the scrolls in all their mysterious beauty, we offer the library's welcome to a trip that takes us back two thousand years to a past all of us share.

M. H. de Young Memorial Museum

Harry S. Parker III
Director
Fine Arts Museums
of San Francisco

We are delighted to welcome Scrolls from the Dead Sea to the Fine Arts Museums of San Francisco. The exhibition at the M. H. de Young Memorial Museum marks the first opportunity the people of the Bay Area have had to see these exciting works of great cultural significance. Although they are not works of art themselves, the scrolls offer the promise of greater understanding of Judaism and the origins of Christianity, which inspired many great works of art.

Antiquities have played an important role in this museum since its founding, both in special exhibitions and as important elements of our permanent collection. During the past twenty years, major exhibitions such as The Vatican Collections: The Papacy and Art, The Search for Alexander, and Treasures of Tutankhamun gave Bay Area viewers a look at the art and culture of Rome, Greece, and ancient Egypt. Scrolls from the Dead Sea offers a glimpse of a different culture, one that is equally a cornerstone of Western civilization.

Scholarship is the common ground between this exhibition and the art museum. Art historians, whether striving to understand and interpret the art of long ago or of today, follow similar paths and require the same profound depth of knowledge as biblical scholars struggling to piece together the clues hidden in the Dead Sea Scrolls. Each new step these scholars take, whether presented as an exhibition or in some other way, offers the public the opportunity for greater understanding of our past and present.

Many people have been involved in realizing Scrolls from the Dead Sea in San Francisco. Our thanks must go first and foremost to Bernard and Barbara Osher and the Osher Foundation, whose enthusiastic support made it possible to bring the exhibition to San Francisco. I would also like to extend my thanks to Delta Air Lines, the official airline of the exhibition, for its valuable contribution. On the staff of the Fine Arts Museums, particular recognition must go to Steven Nash, associate director and chief curator; Melissa Leventon, acting curator of textiles and curator for this exhibition; and Renée Beller Dreyfus, curator for interpretation and antiquities. It has been our pleasure to collaborate with our colleagues in New York, Jerusalem, and Washington, D.C.; I would like to express my gratitude to Irene Burnham and Michael W. Grunberger at the Library of Congress, Ayala Sussmann and Ruth Peled at the Israel Antiquities Authority, and Susan F. Saidenberg and Leonard S. Gold at the New York Public Library for sharing with us their vision and expertise.

W hen I was barely ten years old, the discovery of the Dead Sea Scrolls was front-page news in our local newspaper. These stories were the stuff that set a young boy dreaming. An ancient world—artifacts from which our contemporary biblical printed word, concepts, and religious beliefs were drawn—was suddenly made real to millions of us. When the caves at Qumran were opened, mysteries began to unravel, fascinating everyone from scholars to children.

The Israel Antiquities Authority deserves great credit for having inspired this exhibition. Even though resources are dear, Gen. Amir Drori, his able associate Jacob Fisch, and their colleagues have been unstinting in their assistance. Their cooperation has allowed our talented partners at the Library of Congress, Michael W. Grunberger, Doris A. Hamburg, and Irene Burnham and their staffs, to develop a highly educational, beautifully designed exhibition.

Librarian of Congress James H. Billington, with whom we previously had the pleasure of working to allow the public to see the jewels of the Library's Hebraic collection, deserves public tribute and gratitude. He has been devoted to making sure the American people have full access to all the treasures of our great national library. When David Peleg of the Embassy of Israel asked me whether Dr. Billington would consider hosting this exhibition of the Dead Sea Scrolls, it took only as long as a return telephone call for Dr. Billington to agree enthusiastically.

Public recognition and thanks are due Bernard and Barbara Osher of San Francisco. These modest, gentle persons responded with enthusiasm and alacrity to provide the critical principal funding. Their generosity allowed the entire complicated exhibition process to advance at an unusually rapid pace without sacrificing quality and dignity.

Others were inspired by the Oshers' example, providing funding that completed what otherwise could have been an impossible process in a difficult economic environment. The Jewish Community Federation/Louis Dessauer Trust of San Francisco and the Jewish Community Endowment Fund of the Jewish Community Federation of San Francisco, the Peninsula, Marin and Sonoma Counties each contributed generously to make this exhibition a reality.

The United Jewish Endowment Fund of the UJA Federation of Greater Washington has always participated early on beginning with our first major exhibition, The Precious Legacy, as well as with From the Ends of the Earth: Judaic Treasures of the Library of Congress, and now with Scrolls from the Dead Sea. Melvin and Ryna Cohen also have been stalwarts, responding with assistance when it was most needed. George and Phyllis Cohen have been enthusiastic in their support. Arlene and Raymond Zimmerman have been partners in each endeavor, knowing how much their support counts each time. Rhoda and Richard Goldman's support is gratefully acknowledged here, for all that they do is good.

Lemmon Company's assistance is most welcome, and Marc A. Goshko's

PROJECT JUDAICA FOUNDATION

Mark E. Talisman
President

efforts most appreciated. We are pleased also to acknowledge the support for this project shown by the Zabludowicz Trust.

Phyllis Cook, with whom I have had the long joy of working, is a person of vision who really cares about quality. Her unstinting advice and assistance were crucial in bringing the Dead Sea Scrolls to the American public. Wayne Feinstein was helpful to this entire process as well.

A number of very close friends continue to help. They are Lauren and Joel Jacob, Morey and Sondra Myers, Frank Ridge, Norman and Dulcie Rosenfeld, and Alyn and Marlyn Essman.

Father Timothy Healy, the late president of the New York Public Library, was a friend of very long standing. His untimely death has truly caused a void that will not be filled. Yet his vision in agreeing to host the exhibition of the scrolls at the library was typical of his commitment to scholarship and public access. His last written words found among these pages demonstrate how important he was to us all and how much he will be missed.

Harry S. Parker III quickly agreed to exhibit the scrolls at the M. H. de Young Memorial Museum, one of the highly acclaimed Fine Arts Museums of San Francisco, which he directs. By doing so he guarantees that thousands of visitors to his great institution on the West Coast will enjoy this learning experience. We are all most grateful.

My colleagues on the board of the Project Judaica Foundation, who also are close friends, have helped realize other impossible dreams to allow children and their parents to learn by seeing real objects of history. Sandra Weiner, Sam Golman, Arnold C. Greenberg, and David Farber are powerful forces for good. I know that they sometimes dread hearing from me, yet they still respond with good humor and effectiveness. Patrick McMahon, executive director of the foundation, has skillfully and quietly supported all our efforts.

Most of all, my wife, Jill, deserves accolades for having endured long nights as I sought to accomplish the goals of yet another worthy project. But she was always enthusiastic, and the support of our two children, Jessica and Raphael, made the project's goals easier to reach.

Too often our society has reduced support for cultural endeavors when understandable human service needs had to be met. Yet when our children have the opportunity to dream dreams through such cultural experiences—understanding where we all have come from—the future of our country is brighter and more assured. The realization of this exhibition is a great tribute to those who provided the funds, each of whom recognizes the importance of nurturing the minds and souls of our people as we continue to strive to guarantee their futures.

LIBRARY OF CONGRESS

Project Judaica Foundation gratefully acknowledges the special assistance of the following individuals and institutions:

PRINCIPAL SPONSOR
Bernard Osher Jewish Philanthropies Foundation

PATRONS
The Jewish Community Federation/ Louis Dessauer Trust

Jewish Community Endowment Fund of the Jewish Community Federation of San Francisco, the Peninsula, Marin and Sonoma Counties

BENEFACTORS
Melvin and Ryna Cohen

United Jewish Endowment Fund of the UJA Federation of Greater Washington

Raymond Zimmerman Family Foundation

DONORS
Richard N. and Rhoda H. Goldman Philanthropic Fund

LEMMON Company/ TEVA Pharmaceuticals Industries, Ltd.

Zabludowicz Trust

Ruth and Harold Roitenberg

Farber Family Foundation

Ann E. Sheffer

CONTRIBUTORS
George and Phyllis Cohen

Clyde and Estelle Duneier

The Alyn and Marlyn Essman Philanthropic Fund

Mae S. Gelb

Joel and Lauren Jacob

Morey and Sondra Myers

Frank Ridge

Norman and Dulcie Rosenfeld

DONORS TO THE EXHIBITION

NEW YORK PUBLIC LIBRARY

The New York venue of this exhibition is made possible through the generosity of Republic National Bank of New York and an anonymous donor.

Republic National Bank of New York has had a long-standing commitment to arts and culture. Support of this exhibition is the most recent example of that commitment.

Edmond J. Safra, founder and honorary chairman of Republic National Bank of New York, whose family origins lie in the Middle East,

is particularly pleased to be associated with these important historic treasures that bear witness to the lives of the Jewish people in their land two thousand years ago and sustain their relevance to people of all faiths today.

Republic National Bank of New York seeks to bring arts and culture to the widest possible audience, as evidenced by its support of major historical and artistic exhibitions in the United States and abroad, including Circa 1492, Frans Hals, and Berthe Morisot—Impressionist

at the National Gallery of Art in Washington; Andrew Wyeth and Sickert Paintings at the Royal Academy in London; and D'une Main Forte, a collection of Hebraic manuscripts at the 1991 Paris Exhibition.

Republic National Bank of New York is honored to be associated with this extraordinary historic exhibition of the Dead Sea Scrolls and wishes to thank the Israel Antiquities Authority, the Library of Congress, and the New York Public Library for their scholarship and enthusiasm.

This exhibition is supported by an indemnity from the Federal Council on the Arts and the Humanities.

Delta Air Lines is the official carrier of this exhibition.

Additional support has been received from Hilton International.

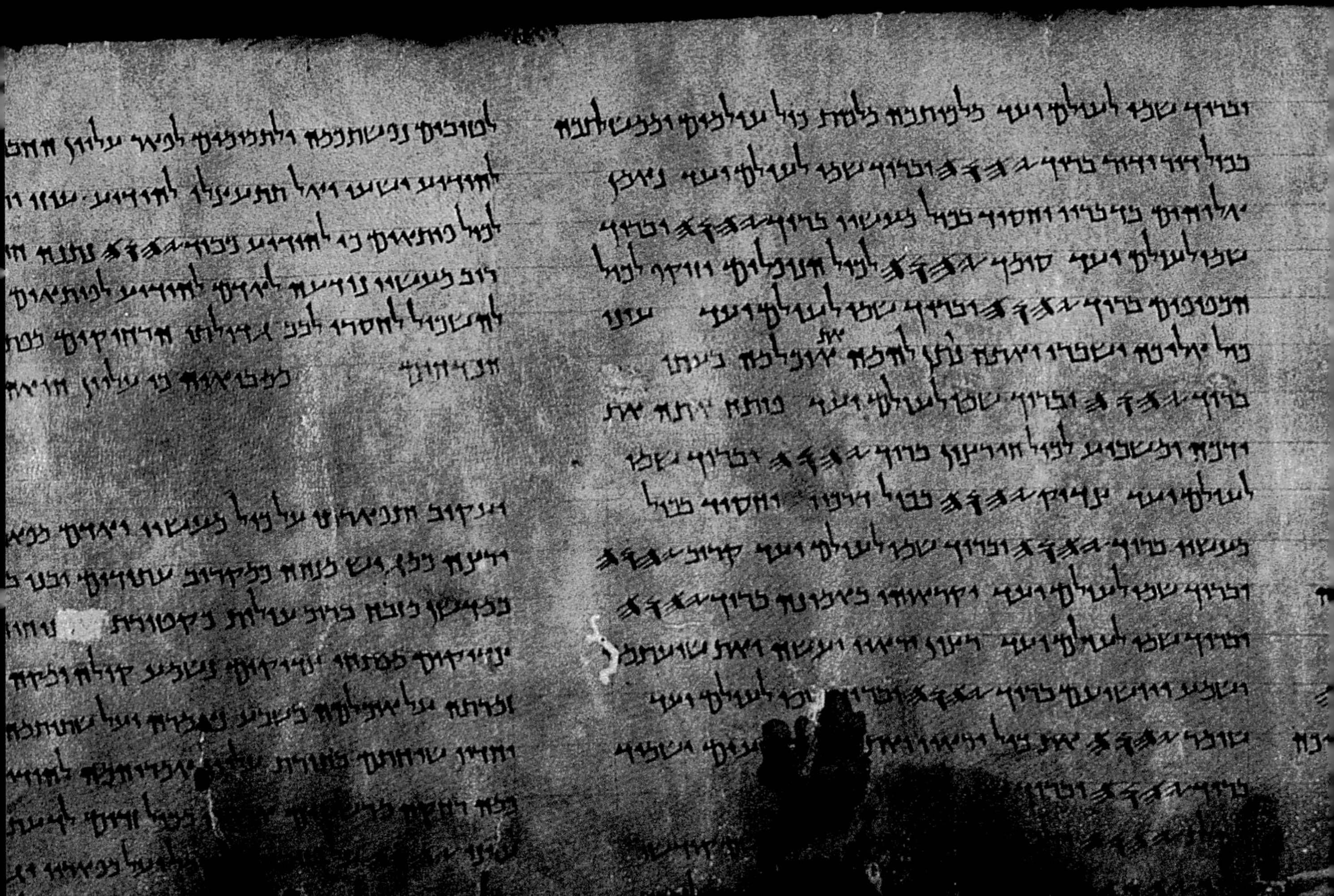

THE DEAD SEA SCROLLS

For the past several years the Dead Sea Scrolls have been the subject of intense public interest. Newspaper and television reports have chronicled—and fueled—the controversy surrounding the slow pace of scroll publication. The "liberation" of the scrolls occurred in late 1991, as unauthorized microfilms, photographic reproductions, and computer-driven reconstructions were made widely available.

The publication controversy is rooted in the special circumstances surrounding the acquisition of the scrolls. Within a decade of their discovery in 1947 all the scrolls but one (the Temple Scroll) had been uncovered and were housed in two Jerusalem repositories, one located in territory controlled by Israel and the other in territory controlled by Jordan. The scrolls in Israeli hands—larger and more intact—were published in short order.

When hostilities ceased in 1949 an intensive search for more scrolls was mounted. Eleven scroll caves were discovered. By far the most important was Cave 4, which contained thousands of fragments from hundreds of compositions. They were removed to the Rockefeller Museum, where they were sorted and stored between glass plates. The myriad fragments were first sorted into compositions and then organized further according to scribal hand. This task fell to an eight-member team of scholars formed in 1953 as the official publication group, led by Pére Roland de Vaux, head of the École Biblique in Jerusalem. No Jewish or Israeli scholars were invited to join the team.

The work proceeded slowly. The first volume of Discoveries in the Judaean Desert, the official publication series, was released in 1955. Volumes II and III appeared in 1961 and 1962 respectively. In 1965, with the publication of the Psalms Scroll (catalog no. 5) as Volume IV, the series title was changed to Discoveries in the Judaean Desert of Jordan, adding a dash of politics to the already volatile mix. The fifth volume, which was in press in 1967 and published in 1968, also carried this series title. In the wake of the 1967 Arab-Israeli War, the Rockefeller Museum building came under Israeli control, but the authorities chose to honor the original arrangements. The pace of publication slowed even further. Volume VI took a decade to complete, appearing only in 1977.

That year scholar Geza Vermes warned that "unless drastic measures are taken at once, the greatest and most valuable of all . . . Hebrew and Aramaic manuscript discoveries is likely to become the academic scandal par excellence of the twentieth century." His warning was not heeded: It took five years to publish Volume VII, and Volume VIII appeared eight years later, in 1990. Hershel Shanks, editor of *Biblical Archaeology Review,* took up the cause in the mid-1980s, using his popular magazine to attack restricted access to the manuscripts.

In 1988 Gen. Amir Drori was appointed head of the Israel Department of Antiquities (later Israel Antiquities Authority). Emanuel Tov, an Israeli scholar, was designated editor-in-chief of the scroll publication committee. Under his direction deadlines were set and the number of scholars with scroll assignments grew from eight to more than fifty.

Despite these steps public pressure increased as Hershel Shanks and others recast the issue as one of intellectual freedom and the right of all scholars — not just members of the scroll "cartel" — to have access to the scrolls. Editorials supporting his position appeared in newspapers across America. Some persons even asserted that access was restricted because the scrolls contained untold secrets that, once revealed, would undermine the foundations of established religions. The Israel Antiquities Authority believed that the steps already taken would lay to rest the issue by the year 2000.

As often happens, however, events overtook debate. In the fall of 1991 the Huntington Library announced that it would make available to scholars security copies of photographs of the scrolls deposited in its vaults. Next, two Hebrew Union College scholars developed a computer program that reconstructed Cave 4 texts from a decades-old concordance. The first fascicle of the reconstructions was published in late 1991, as was a two-volume edition of scroll photographs. Both the computer reconstruction and the facsimile edition were issued by the Biblical Archaeology Society, headed by Hershel Shanks. Closing the circle, the Israel Antiquities Authority announced that it would be issuing an authorized microfiche edition, complete with detailed indexes.

EXHIBITIONS OF THE DEAD SEA SCROLLS

This exhibition, opening at the Library of Congress and traveling to New York and San Francisco, is not the first in the United States. That occurred in 1949 — also at the Library of Congress. Three scrolls — the Isaiah Scroll, the Habakkuk Commentary, and the Community Rule — were displayed. From the Library the exhibition traveled to the Walters Art Gallery in Baltimore, Duke University, the Oriental Institute of the University of Chicago, and the Worcester Art Museum.

In 1965 the Smithsonian Institution, in cooperation with the government of Jordan and the Palestine Archaeological Museum (the Rockefeller Museum), mounted an international traveling exhibition entitled Scrolls from the Wilderness of the Dead Sea. This exhibition embraced a full range of fragmentary scrolls (including catalog no. 5) as well as related artifacts. From Washington it traveled to Philadelphia, Berkeley, Claremont, Omaha, and Baltimore and then to Ottawa and Toronto and finally to Great Britain.

The exhibit Treasures of the Holy Land, shown at the Metropolitan Museum of Art in 1986–87, included one scroll, the Habakkuk Commentary, from the Shrine of the Book in Jerusalem. The exhibition traveled to Los Angeles and Houston. The New York Public Library included the Nahum Commentary, also from the Shrine of the Book, in its 1988 exhibit A Sign and a Witness: 2,000 Years of Hebrew Books and Illuminated Manuscripts.

ABOUT THIS CATALOG

This exhibition catalog is divided into two main sections. The first, "From the Scroll Caves," describes the twelve scroll fragments included in the exhibition. The second section, "From the Qumran Ruin," presents artifacts excavated at the nearby Qumran ruin in addition to a number of items from the caves.

The curatorial descriptions of the scrolls include the following elements:

1. an exhibit number

2. a translated name for the scroll (e.g., Hosea Commentary)

3. a transliterated name (e.g., Pesher Hoshe'a)

4. the name of the scroll in Hebrew

5. the scroll's classification number. The traditional notation generally includes some or all of the following information: the number of the cave in which the fragment was uncovered; the location of the cave; the number assigned to the overall fragment; an abbreviated name; and the specific fragment number (e.g., the classification number 4QpHos^a would indicate cave 4, Qumran, Pesher Hoshe'a, fragment a).

6. an approximation of the period in which the scroll was copied

7. measurements of the fragment in centimeters and inches

8. a description of the scroll. References to scholarly articles and monographs on the fragment are located at the foot of the entry.

9. a translation of the scroll by a leading scholar as well as a transcription into Hebrew script of a portion of the text. Translated and transcribed text enclosed in brackets indicates letters, words, or passages supplied by the translator or transcriber. Large brackets around the scroll fragments assist the reader in locating the transcribed portions.

The second section of the catalog, "From the Qumran Ruin," describes the archeological artifacts. They are organized by material, such as pottery, wood, leather, and textiles. Brief introductions and captions describe the materials and their uses.

Scrolls from the Dead Sea brings before the American people a selection from the very scrolls that have been the focus of so much recent scrutiny and speculation. It is our hope that this exhibition and catalog will lead to a greater understanding of the turbulent period in which the Dead Sea Scrolls were copied—a period that set the stage for the emergence of modern Judaism and Christianity. It is our hope also that this exhibition will encourage a better understanding of the challenges and complexities connected with scroll research. We have aimed to create a realistic expectation of the potential fruits of scroll research as well as an appreciation for the considerable patience, skill, and persistence of those charged with gathering the harvest.

Abbreviations

B.C.E.	Before the Common Era, an alternate designation for B.C.
C.E.	Common Era, an alternate designation for A.D.
ca.	*Circa,* about or around a date
vacat	Space left intentionally by the scribe

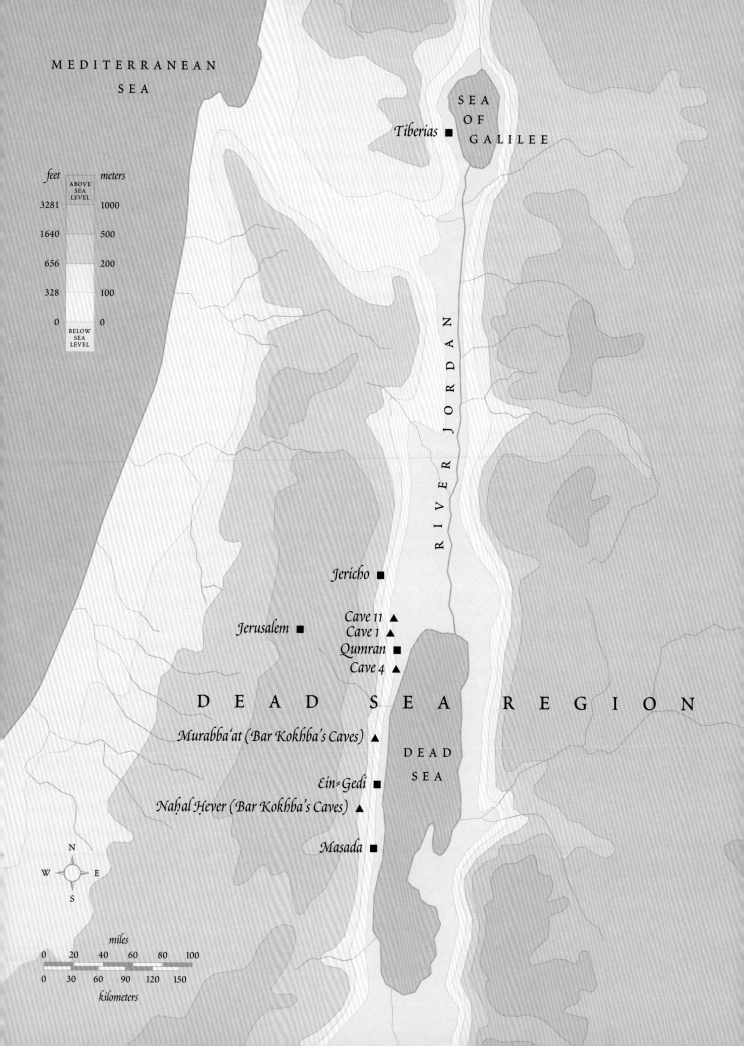

MEDITERRANEAN
SEA

SEA
OF
GALILEE

Tiberias ■

feet   meters

ABOVE
SEA
LEVEL

3281   1000

1640   500

656   200

328   100

0   0

BELOW
SEA
LEVEL

RIVER JORDAN

Jericho ■

Cave 11 ▲
Cave 1 ▲
Qumran ■
Cave 4 ▲

Jerusalem ■

D E A D   S E A   R E G I O N

Murabba'at (Bar Kokhba's Caves) ▲

DEAD
SEA

Ein-Gedi ■

Naḥal Ḥever (Bar Kokhba's Caves) ▲

Masada ■

N
W   E
S

miles

0   20   40   60   80   100

0   30   60   90   120   150

kilometers

Ancient Hebrew scrolls accidentally discovered in 1947 by a Bedouin boy have kindled popular enthusiasm as well as serious scholarly interest over the past half century. The source of this excitement is what these Dead Sea Scrolls reveal about the history of the Second Temple period (520 B.C.E.–70 C.E.), particularly from the second century B.C.E. until the destruction of the Second Temple in 70 C.E.—a time of crucial developments in the crystallization of the monotheistic religions.

The Judean Desert, a region reputedly barren, defied preconceptions and yielded an unprecedented treasure. The young Taʿamireh shepherd was certainly unaware of destiny when his innocent search for a stray goat led to the fateful discovery of Hebrew scrolls in a long-untouched cave. One discovery led to another, and eleven scroll-yielding caves and a habitation site eventually were uncovered. Since 1947 the site of these discoveries—the Qumran region (the desert plain and the adjoining mountainous ridge) and the Qumran site—have been subjected to countless probes; not a stone has remained unturned in the desert, not an aperture unprobed. The Qumran settlement has been exhaustively excavated.

The first trove found by the Bedouins in the Judean Desert consisted of seven large scrolls from Cave 1. The unusual circumstances of the find, on the eve of Israel's war of independence, obstructed the initial negotiations for the purchase of all the scrolls. Shortly before the establishment of the state of Israel, Professor E. L. Sukenik of the Hebrew University clandestinely acquired three of the scrolls from a Christian Arab antiquities dealer in Bethlehem. The remaining four scrolls reached the hands of Mar Athanasius Yeshua Samuel, Metropolitan of the Syrian Jacobite Monastery of St. Mark in Jerusalem. In 1949 he traveled to the United States with the scrolls, but five years went by before the prelate found a purchaser.

On June 1, 1954, Mar Samuel placed an advertisement in the *Wall Street Journal* offering "The Four Dead Sea Scrolls" for sale. The advertisement was brought to the attention of Yigael Yadin, Professor Sukenik's son, who had just retired as chief of staff of the Israel Defense Forces and had reverted to his primary vocation, archeology. With the aid of intermediaries, the four scrolls were purchased from Mar Samuel for $250,000. Thus, the scrolls that had eluded Yadin's father because of the war were now at his disposal. Part of the purchase price was contributed by D. S. Gottesman, a New York philanthropist. His heirs sponsored construction of the Shrine of the Book in Jerusalem's Israel Museum, in which these unique manuscripts are exhibited to the public.

The seven scrolls from Cave 1, now housed together in the Shrine of the Book, are Isaiah A, Isaiah B, the Habakkuk Commentary, the Thanksgiving Scroll, the Community Rule (or the Manual of Discipline), the War Rule (or the War of Sons of Light Against the Sons of Darkness), and the Genesis Apocryphon, the last being in Aramaic. All the large scrolls have been published.

TREASURES FROM THE JUDEAN DESERT

Ayala Sussmann and Ruth Peled

The Caves. At least a year elapsed between the discovery of the scrolls in 1947 and the initiation of a systematic archeological investigation of the Qumran site. The northern Dead Sea area, the location of Qumran, became and remained part of Jordan until 1967. The search for scroll material rested in the hands of the Bedouins, who ravaged the Cave 1 site, no doubt losing precious material in the process.

Early in 1949 the cave site was finally identified by the archeological authorities of Jordan. G. Lankester Harding, director of the Jordanian Antiquities Department, undertook to excavate Cave 1 with Pére Roland de Vaux, a French Dominican priest who headed the École Biblique in Jerusalem. Exploration of the cave, which lay one kilometer north of Wadi Qumran, yielded at least seventy fragments, including bits of the original seven scrolls. This discovery established the provenance of the purchased scrolls. Also recovered were archeological artifacts that confirmed the scroll dates suggested by paleographic study.

The Bedouins continued to search for scrolls, as these scraps of leather proved to be a fine source of income. Because Cave 1 had been exhausted by archeological excavation, the fresh material that the Bedouins were offering proved that Cave 1 was not an isolated phenomenon in the desert and that other caves with manuscripts also existed.

The years between 1951 and 1956 were marked by accelerated activity in both the search for caves and the archeological excavation of sites related to the manuscripts. An eight-kilometer-long strip of cliffs was thoroughly investigated. Of the eleven caves that yielded manuscripts, five were discovered by the Bedouins and six by archeologists. Some of the caves were particularly rich in material. Cave 3 preserved two oxidized rolls of beaten copper (the Copper Scroll), containing a lengthy roster of real or imaginary hidden treasures—a tantalizing enigma to this day. Cave 4 was particularly rich in material: 15,000 fragments from at least six hundred composite texts were found there. The last manuscript cave discovered, Cave 11, was located in 1956, providing extensive documents, including the Psalms Scroll (catalog no. 5), an Aramaic *targum* of Job, and the Temple Scroll, the longest (about twenty-nine feet) of the Qumran manuscripts. The Temple Scroll was acquired by Yigael Yadin in 1967 and is now housed alongside the first seven scrolls in the Shrine of the Book at the Israel Museum in Jerusalem. All the remaining manuscripts, sizable texts as well as minute fragments, are stored in the Rockefeller Museum building in Jerusalem, the premises of the Israel Antiquities Authority.

Khirbet Qumran (The Qumran Ruin). Pére de Vaux gradually realized the need to identify a habitation site close to the caves. Excavating such a site could provide clues that would help identify the people who deposited the scrolls.

The ruins of Qumran lie on a barren terrace between the limestone cliffs of the Judean Desert and the maritime bed along the Dead Sea. The excavations uncovered a complex of structures, 262 by 328 feet (80 by 100 meters), pre-

Mar Samuel's 1954 advertisement in the Wall Street Journal *attracted attention and eventually a buyer.*

Plates, bowls, and goblets were found in one room at Qumran, with dozens of vessels piled one on top of the other. This room probably served as a crockery near the assembly room, which may have been a dining room.

served to a considerable height. The structures were neither military nor private but rather communal in character.

Nearby were remains of burials. Pottery uncovered was identical with that of Cave 1 and confirmed the link with the nearby caves. Following the initial excavations, de Vaux suggested that this site was the wilderness retreat established by the Essene sect, which was alluded to by ancient historians. The sectarians inhabited neighboring locations, most likely caves, tents, and solid structures, but depended on the center for communal facilities such as stores of food and water. Excavations conducted in 1956 and 1958 at the neighboring site of 'En Feshkha proved it to be the agricultural adjunct of Qumran.

The final report on the Qumran settlement excavations is pending, but the results are known through preliminary publications.

The discovery of the Dead Sea Scrolls caused heated controversy in scholarly circles over their date and the identity of the community they represented.

DATING OF THE SCROLLS

Professor Sukenik, after initially defining the time span of the scrolls as the Second Temple period, recognized their special significance and advocated the now widely accepted theory that they were remnants of the library of the Essenes. At the time, however, he was vociferously opposed by a number of scholars who doubted the antiquity as well as the authenticity of the texts. Lingering in the memory of learned circles was the notorious Shapira affair of 1883. M. Shapira, a Jerusalem antiquities dealer, announced the discovery of an ancient text of Deuteronomy. His texts, allegedly inscribed on fifteen leather strips, caused a huge stir in Europe and were even exhibited at the British Museum. Shortly thereafter, the leading European scholars of the day denounced the writings as rank forgeries.

Today scholarly opinion regarding the time span and background of the Dead Sea Scrolls is anchored in historical, paleographic, and linguistic evidence, corroborated firmly by carbon 14 datings. Some manuscripts were written and copied in the third century B.C.E., but the bulk of the material, particularly the texts that reflect on a sectarian community, are originals or copies from the first century B.C.E.; a number of texts date from as late as the years preceding the destruction of the site in 68 C.E. at the hands of the Roman legions.

THE ESSENES

The Qumran sect's origins are postulated by some scholars to be in the communities of the *Hasidim,* the pious anti-Hellenistic circles formed in the early days of the Maccabees. The *Hasidim* may have been the precursors of the Essenes, who were concerned about growing Hellenization and strove to abide by the Torah.

Archeological and historical evidence indicates that Qumran was founded in the second half of the second century B.C.E., during the time of the Maccabean dynasty. A hiatus in the occupation of the site is linked to evidence of a huge earthquake. Qumran was abandoned about the time of the Roman incursion of 68 C.E., two years before the collapse of Jewish self-government in Judea and the destruction of the Temple in Jerusalem in 70 C.E.

The chief sources of information for the history of this fateful time span are the Qumran scrolls and the excavations, but earlier information on the Essenes was provided by their contemporaries: Josephus Flavius, Philo of Alexandria, and Pliny the Elder. Their accounts are continuously being borne out by the site excavations and study of the writings.

The historian Josephus relates the division of the Jews of the Second Temple period into three orders: the Sadducees, the Pharisees, and the Essenes. The Sadducees included mainly the priestly and aristocratic families; the Pharisees constituted the lay circles; and the Essenes were a separatist group, part of which formed an ascetic monastic community that retreated to the wilderness. The exact political and religious affinities of each of these groups, as well as their development and interrelationships, are still relatively obscure and are the source of widely disparate scholarly views.

The crisis that brought about the secession of the Essenes from mainstream Judaism is thought to have occurred when the Maccabean ruling princes Jonathan (160–142 B.C.E.) and Simeon (142–134 B.C.E.) usurped the office of high priest (which included secular duties), much to the consternation of conservative Jews; some of them could not tolerate the situation and denounced the new rulers. The persecution of the Essenes and their leader, the "teacher of righteousness," probably elicited the sect's apocalyptic visions. These included the overthrow of "the wicked priest" of Jerusalem and of the evil people and, in the dawn of the Messianic Age, the recognition of their community as the true Israel. The retreat of these Jews into the desert would enable them "to separate themselves from the congregation of perverse men" (1Q Serekh 5:2).

A significant feature of the Essene sect is its calendar, which was based on a solar system of 364 days, unlike the common Jewish calendar, which was lunar and consisted of 354 days. It is not clear how the sectarian calendar was reconciled, as was the normative Jewish calendar, with the astronomical time system (see catalog no. 10).

The sectarian calendar was always reckoned from a Wednesday, the day on which God created the luminaries. The year consisted of fifty-two weeks, divided into four seasons of thirteen weeks each, and the festivals consistently fell on the same days of the week. A similar solar system was long familiar from pseudepigraphic works. The sectarian calendar played a weighty role in the schism of the community from the rest of Judaism, as the festivals and fast days of the sect were ordinary work days for the mainstream community and vice versa. The author of the Book of Jubilees accuses the followers of the lunar calendar of turning secular "days of impurity" into "festivals and holy days" (Jubilees 6:36–37).

The Essenes persisted in a separatist existence through two centuries, occupying themselves with study and a communal way of life that included worship, prayer, and work. It is clear, however, that large groups of adherents also lived in towns and villages outside the Qumran area.

The word *Essene* is never distinctly mentioned in the scrolls. How then can we attribute either the writings or the sites of the Judean Desert to the Essenes?

The argument in favor of this ascription is supported by the tripartite division of Judaism referred to in Qumran writings (for example, in the Nahum Commentary) into Ephraim, Menasseh, and Judah, corresponding to the Pharisees, the Sadducees, and the Essenes. As the Essenes refer to themselves in the scrolls as Judah, it is quite clear whom they regarded themselves to be. Moreover, their religious concepts and beliefs as attested in the scrolls conform to those recorded by contemporary writers and stand in sharp contrast to those of the other known Jewish groups.

In most cases the principles of the Essene way of life and beliefs are described by contemporaneous writers in language similar to the self-descriptions found in the scrolls. Customs described in ancient sources as Essene—such as the probationary period for new members, the strict hierarchy practiced in the organization of the sect, their frequent ablutions, and communal meals—are all echoed in the scrolls. From the Community Rule: "Communally they shall eat and communally they shall bless and communally they shall take counsel" (1Q Serekh 6:1). Finally, the location of the sect is assigned to the Dead Sea area by the Roman historian Pliny the Elder.

Although this evidence is accepted by the majority of scholars as conclusive in identifying the Essenes with the Qumran settlement and the manuscripts found in the surrounding caves, a number of scholars remain vehemently opposed. Some propose that the site was a military garrison or even a winter villa. The scrolls are viewed as an eclectic collection, neither necessarily inscribed in

the Dead Sea area nor sectarian in nature, perhaps even the remains of the library of the Temple in Jerusalem. Other scholars view the texts as the writings of forerunners or even followers of Jesus—Jewish Christians—who still observed Jewish law.

The Qumran Library

The collection of writings recovered in the Qumran environs has restored to us a voluminous corpus of Jewish documents dating from the third century B.C.E. to 68 C.E., demonstrating the rich literary activity of Second Temple–period Jewry. The collection comprises documents of a varied nature, most of them of a distinct religious bent. The chief categories represented are biblical, apocryphal or pseudepigraphical, and sectarian writings. The study of this original library has demonstrated that the boundaries between these categories are far from clear-cut.

The biblical manuscripts include what are probably the earliest copies of these texts to have come down to us. Most of the books of the Bible are represented in the collection. Some books are extant in a large number of copies; others are represented only fragmentarily on mere scraps of parchment. The biblical texts display considerable similarity to the standard Masoretic (received) text. This, however, is not always the rule, and many texts diverge from the Masoretic. For example, some of the texts of Samuel from Cave 4 follow the Septuagint, the Greek version of the Bible translated in the third to second centuries B.C.E. Indeed, Qumran has yielded copies of the Septuagint in Greek.

The biblical scrolls in general have provided many new readings that facilitate the reconstruction of the textual history of the Old Testament. It is also significant that several manuscripts of the Bible, including the Leviticus Scroll (catalog no. 4), are inscribed not in the Jewish script dominant at the time but rather in the ancient paleo-Hebrew script.

A considerable number of apocryphal and pseudepigraphic texts are preserved at Qumran, where original Hebrew and Aramaic versions of these Jewish compositions of the Second Temple period were first encountered. These writings, which are not included in the canonical Jewish scriptures, were preserved by different Christian churches and were transmitted in Greek, Ethiopic, Syriac, Armenian, and other translations.

Some of these are narrative texts closely related to biblical compositions, such as the Book of Jubilees and Enoch (catalog no. 11), whereas others are independent works—for example, Tobit and Ben Sira. Apparently some of these compositions were treated by the Qumran community as canonical and were studied by them.

The most original and unique group of writings from Qumran are the sectarian ones, which were practically unknown until their discovery in 1947. An exception is the Damascus Document (or Damascus Covenant), which lacked a definite identification before the discoveries of the Dead Sea area (see catalog no. 1). This widely varied literature reveals the beliefs and customs of a pietistic commune, probably centered at Qumran, and includes rules and ordinances, biblical commentaries, apocalyptic visions, and liturgical works, generally attributed to the last quarter of the second century B.C.E. and onward.

The "rules," the collections of rules and instructions reflecting the practices of the commune, are exemplified by the Damascus Document (catalog no. 1), the Community Rule (catalog no. 7), and Some Torah Precepts (catalog no. 8). Here we witness a considerable corpus of legal material *(Halakhah)* that has much in common with the rabbinic tradition preserved at a later date in the Mishnah. The *Halakhah* emerging from the sectarian writings seems to be corroborated by the sectarian *Halakhah* referred to in rabbinic sources.

The biblical commentaries *(pesharim)*, such as the Habakkuk Commentary, the Nahum Commentary, and the Hosea Commentary (catalog no. 6), are attested solely at Qumran and grew out of the sect's eschatological presuppositions. The Scriptures were scanned by the sect for allusions to current and future events. These allusions could be understood only by the sectarians themselves, because only they possessed "eyes to see"—their distinct eschatological vision. Liturgical works figure prominently among the sectarian manuscripts at Qumran because of the centrality of prayer in this period. The Thanksgiving Psalms *(Hodayot)* are of two types: those characterized by a personal tone, attributed by some to the "teacher of righteousness," and the communal type, referring to a group.

Many more compositions deserve mention, but this brief survey demonstrates the major role played by the Dead Sea Scrolls in improving our comprehension of this pivotal moment in Jewish history.

LITERARY MILESTONES

← *ca. 6th century* B.C.E. *Canonization of the Torah (Pentateuch), the first of the three major divisions of the Hebrew Bible*

← *ca. 4th century* B.C.E. *Canonization of the Nevi'im (Prophets), the second of the three major divisions of the Hebrew Bible*

← *ca. mid-3rd century* B.C.E. *Completion of the Septuagint (translation of the Pentateuch into Greek)*

ca. 200 B.C.E.–*100* C.E. *Apocryphal and Apocalyptic literature*

KEY FIGURES

POLITICAL AND MILITARY EVENTS

← *586* B.C.E. *Babylonians destroy Jerusalem; beginning of Babylonian exile*

← *538* B.C.E. *Cyrus, ruler of Babylon, permits exiles to return to Judea*

← *333* B.C.E. *Alexander the Great extends Greek rule to Palestine and Egypt*

← *323* B.C.E. *Alexander's empire divided into three parts: Antigonids in Macedonia, Seleucids in Syria, and Ptolemies in Egypt*

← *301* B.C.E. *Ptolemies' rule over Judea begins*

← *198* B.C.E. *Seleucids' rule over Judea begins*

← *168* B.C.E. *Hasmonean revolt*

← *164* B.C.E. *Temple purified by Judas Maccabeus*

THE HASMONEAN DYNASTY

Aristobulus 104–103 B.C.E.

Alexander Jannaeus 103–76 B.C.E.

Judas Maccabeus 166–160 B.C.E.

Salome Alexandra 76–67 B.C.

Jonathan 160–142 B.C.E.

Aristobulus II 67–63 B.C.

Simeon 142–134 B.C.E.

Hyrcanus II 63–40 B.C.E.

John Hyrcanus 134–104 B.C.E.

Antigonus II 40–37 B.C.E.

BEFORE THE COMMON ERA

| 160 | 150 | 140 | 130 | 120 | 110 | 100 | 90 | 80 | 70 | 60 | 50 | 4 |

ca. 40–50 C.E. Beginnings of the New Testament

ca. 90 C.E. Canonization of the Ketuvim (Hagiographa), the third of the three major divisions of the Hebrew Bible →

ca. 200 C.E. Mishnah edited by Rabbi Judah the Prince →

Hillel ca. 80 B.C.E.–ca. 9 C.E.

Philo of Alexandria ca. 30 B.C.E.–45 C.E.

Jesus of Nazareth ca. 4 B.C.E.–29 C.E.

Pontius Pilate procurator of Judea 26–36 C.E.

Josephus Flavius ca. 38–100 C.E.

37 B.C.E. Herod conquers Jerusalem

6–41 C.E. Judea, Samaria, and
Idumea placed under procurators

44–66 C.E. Rule of the procurators

63 C.E. Rome occupies Jerusalem

66 C.E. Revolt against Rome

ca. 68 C.E. Roman legions destroy the Qumran settlement

70 C.E. Roman legions conquer Jerusalem

73 C.E. Masada falls to Rome

THE HERODIAN DYNASTY

Herod the Great 37–4 B.C.E.

Archelaus 4 B.C.E.–6 C.E.

Herod Antipas 4 B.C.E.–39 C.E.

Herod Philip 4 B.C.E.–34 C.E.

Agrippa I 41–44 C.E.

Agrippa II 50–ca. 92 C.E.

THE COMMON ERA

| 30 | 20 | 10 | ◆ | 10 | 20 | 30 | 40 | 50 | 60 | 70 | 80 | 90 |

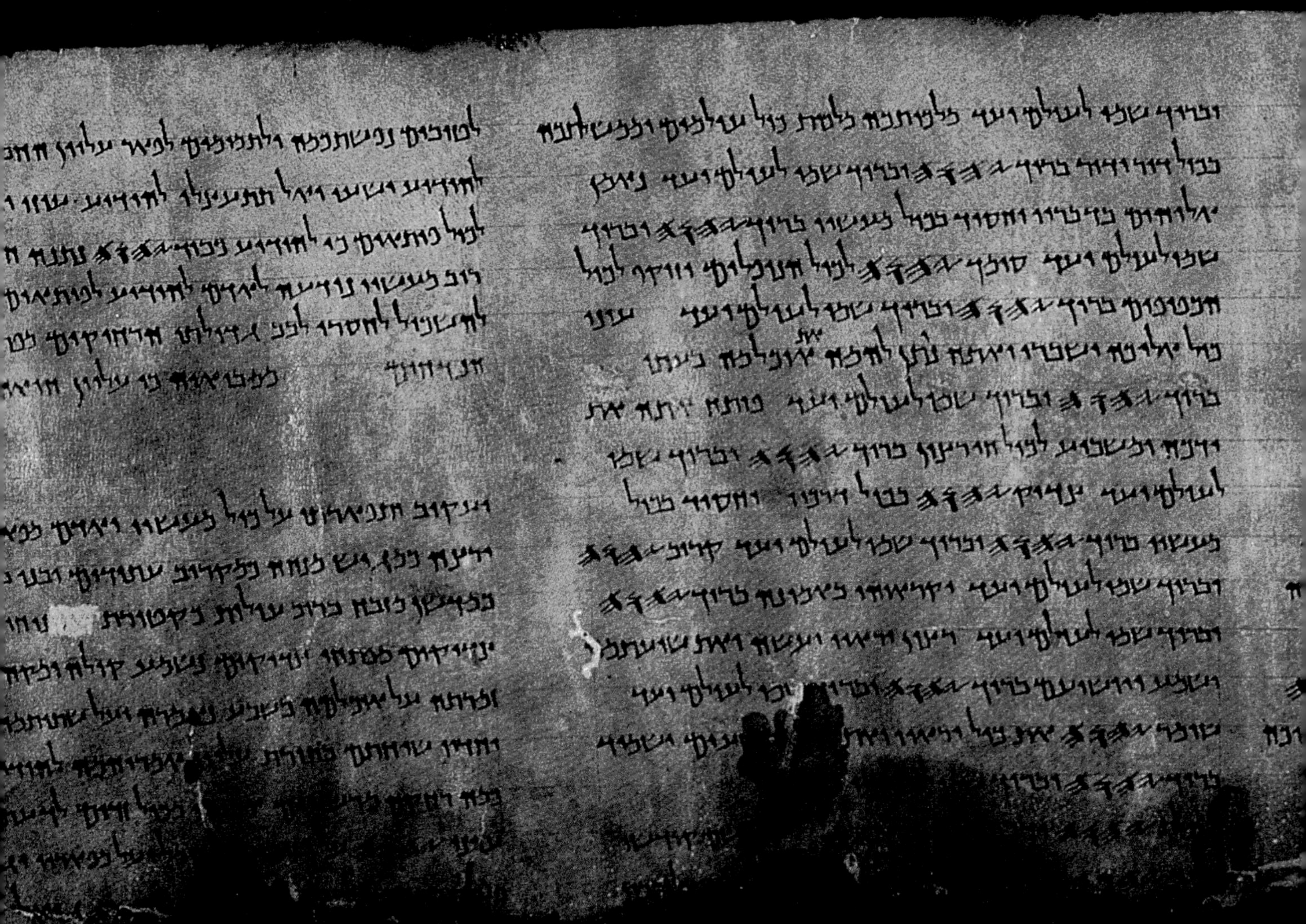

CATALOG

FROM THE
SCROLL CAVES

Solomon Schechter's discovery of the Damascus Document (or Damascus Covenant) in the Cairo Genizah a century ago (see page 28) may be regarded as the true starting point of modern scroll research. In his *Fragments of a Zadokite Work,* published in 1910, he presented two copies of a medieval text that he identified as being of a sectarian nature. Almost a half century passed before inscribed scrolls discovered in the Judean Desert confirmed the Second Temple–period dating that Schechter assigned the text in 1910.

Scholarly controversy has long marked the study of this document, which dates to the late Herodian period (37–4 B.C.E.). Not long after its publication, some scholars began to call it the Damascus Document because it refers to a covenant made in "Damascus." However, the meaning of this name, whether geographical or symbolic (see Amos 5:26), is still debated. As many as seventeen suggestions have been offered as to the identification of the community represented in the Damascus Document, including Zadokites (descendants of the ancient high priest Zadok), Pharisees, Essenes, and early Christians. Only the discovery of similar material in the caves associated with the Qumran site confirmed a link between the Damascus Document and the literature of the Qumran community.

The Damascus Document includes two elements. The first is an admonition that implores the congregation to remain faithful to the covenant of those who retreated from Judea to the "Land of Damascus." The second lists statutes dealing with vows and oaths, the tribunal, witnesses and judges, purification of water, Sabbath laws, and ritual cleanliness.

The order of the ancient Qumran text differs from that of the medieval text found in the Genizah, which also lacks the beginning, the end, and some of the statutes that we are now familiar with through the Qumran text.

One of the eight fragments of the Damascus Document uncovered in Cave 4, the passage displayed here extends the biblical injunction concerning integrity in buying and selling (Lev. 25:14) to the requirement of full disclosure in arranging marriages. Essene men who married took every precaution to ascertain the good moral and physical characters of their wives, as indicated by Josephus (*The Jewish War,* II, 161). This text is not familiar from the Genizah manuscripts and is therefore of great significance.

The right-hand margin is incomplete. The left-hand margin was sewn to another piece of parchment, as evidenced by the remaining stitches.

References

Baumgarten, J. "The Laws of the Damascus Document in Current Research." In *The Damascus Document Reconsidered.* Edited by M. Broshi. Jerusalem, 1992.

Rabin, C. *The Zadokite Documents.* Oxford, 1958.

Schechter, S. *Fragments of a Zadokite Work: Documents of Jewish Sectaries,* vol. 1. Cambridge, England, 1910.

I

DAMASCUS
DOCUMENT
BRIT DAMESEK
ברית דמשק
4Q271(Dᶠ)
Copied late first
century B.C.E.
10.9 × 9.3 cm
(4¼ × 3⅝ in.)

1. . . . with money . . .

2. . . . [his means did not] suffice to [return it to him] and the year
   [for redemption appproaches?] . . .

3. . . . and may God release him? from his sins. Let not [   ] in one, for

4. it is an abomination. . . . And concerning what he said *(Lev. 25:14)*,
   ["When you sell

5. anything to or buy anything from] your neighbor, you shall not defraud
   one another," this is the expli[cation . . .

6. . . .] everything that he knows that is found . . .

7. . . . and he knows that he is wronging him, whether it concerns man or
   beast. And if

8. [a man gives his daughter to another ma]n, let him disclose all her
   blemishes to him, lest he bring upon himself the judgement

9. [of the curse which is said *(Deut. 27:18)*] (of the one) that "makes the
   blind to wander out of the way." Moreover, he should not give her to one
   unfit for her, for

10. [that is Kila'yim, (plowing with) o]x and ass and wearing wool and linen
    together. Let no man bring

11. [a woman into the holy [   ] who has had sexual experience, whether
    she had such experience

12. [in the home] of her father or as a widow who had intercourse after she
    was widowed. And any woman

13. [upon whom] there is a bad name in her maidenhood in her father's
    home, let no man take her, except

14. [upon examination] by reliable [women] who have clear knowledge,
    by command of the Supervisor over

15. [the Many. After]ward he may take her, and when he takes her he shall
    act in accordance with the law . . . and he shall not tell . . .

16. [   ]L[   ]

Transcription and translation by J. Baumgarten

.1   [   ]   [בכסף]

.2   [   ]   [והגי]ן   [   ] וידו לוא ה]שיגה דיו לה]שיב לו   [שנת ה]

.3   [   ]   [עוונותיו   אל]   [ואל יעזוב ל]

.4   [   ]   [באחת כי תועבה היא ואשר אמר כי [תמכור]

.5   [ש[ממכר או קנה מיד] עמיתך לוא תונו איש את עמיתו וזה פרו]ש

.6   תן [   ]   [... בכול אשר הוא יודע אשר ימצא   ]

.7   [   ]   [והוא יודע אשר הוא מועל בו באדם ובבהמה ואם

.8   [בת יתן איש לאי]ש את כול מזמיה יספר לו למה
      יביא עליו את משפט

.9   [הארור אשר אמ]ר משגה עור בדרך וגם אל יתנהה
      לאשר לוא הוכן להכי

.10   [הוא כלאים ש]ור וחמור ולבוש צמר {ופשתים יחדיו אל יבא איש

.11   [אשה ב]   [ם הקו]דש אשר ידעה לעשות מעשה {מדבר ואשר ידעה

.12   [מעשה בבית] אביה או אלמנה אשר נשכבה מאשר התארמלה וכול

.13   [אשר עליה ש]ם רע בבתוליה בבית אביה אל יקחה איש כי אם

.14   [בראות נשים] נאמנות וידעות ברורות ממאמר המבקר אשר על

.15   [הרבים ואח]ר יקחנה ובלוקחו אותה יעשה כמ[ש]פט [ולוא י]גיד ע

.16   [   ]   [ל]   [

The King Jonathan mentioned in this text can be no other than the Hasmonean monarch Alexander Jannaeus (103–76 B.C.E.). His coins, although inscribed in Greek with "King Alexander," have "King Jonathan" in Hebrew.

The discovery of a prayer for the welfare of a Hasmonean king among the Qumran texts is unexpected because the sectarians vehemently opposed the Hasmoneans; they may even have settled in the remote desert to avoid contact with the Hasmonean authorities and priesthood. If this is indeed a composition that clashes with Qumran views, it is a single occurrence among six hundred nonbiblical manuscripts. However, there is a high possibility, perhaps also alluded to in the Nahum Commentary, that Jonathan-Jannaeus, unlike the other Hasmonean rulers, was favored by the Dead Sea sect, at least during certain periods.

This text is unique in that it can be clearly dated to the rule of King Jonathan. Three columns of script are preserved, one on the top and two below. The upper column and the lower left column are incomplete. The leather is torn along the lower third of the right margin. A tab of untanned leather, 2.9 by 2.9 centimeters, folds over the right edge above the tear. A leather thong, remains of which were found threaded through the middle of the tab, probably tied the rolled-up scroll (see catalog nos. 32 and 33 and page 135). The form of the tab—probably part of a fastening—seems to indicate that the extant text was at the beginning of the scroll, which was originally longer. Differences between the script of column A and that of B and C may indicate that the document is not the work of a single scribe.

This small manuscript contains two distinct parts. The first, column A, presents fragments of a psalm of praise to God. The second, columns B and C, bear a prayer for the welfare of King Jonathan and his kingdom. In column A lines 8–10 are similar to a verse in Psalm 154, preserved in the Psalms Scroll (11QPsa, Plate XVIII) exhibited here (catalog no. 5). This hymn, which was not included in the biblical Book of Psalms, is familiar, however, from the tenth-century Syriac Psalter.

Reference

Eshel, E., H. Eshel, and A. Yardeni. "A Qumran Scroll Containing Part of Psalm 154 and a Prayer for the Welfare of King Jonathan and His Kingdom," *Israel Exploration Journal,* forthcoming.

2
PRAYER FOR
KING JONATHAN
TEFILLAH LI-SHLOMO
SHEL YONATAN
HA-MELEKH
תפילה לשלומו
של יונתן המלך
4Q448
Copied 103–76 B.C.E.
17.8 × 9.5 cm
(7 × 3¾ in.)

Column A

1. Praise the Lord, a Psalm [of
2. You loved as a fa[ther(?)
3. you ruled over [
4. *vacat* [
5. and your foes were afraid
   (or: will fear)[
6. … the heaven [
7. and to the depths of the sea [
8. and upon those who glorify
   him [
9. the humble from the hand
   of adversaries [
10. Zion for his habitation,
    ch[ooses

Column C

1. because you love Isr[ael
2. for king Jonathan
3. and all the congregation
   of your people
4. Israel
5. who are in the four
6. winds of heaven
7. peace be (for) all
8. and upon your kingdom
9. your name be blessed

Transcription and translation by
E. Eshel, H. Eshel, and A. Yardeni

Column B

1. holy city
2. in the day and until evening [
3. to approach, to be [
4. Remember them for blessing[
5. on your name, which is called [
6. kingdom to be blessed [
7.]for the day of war [
8. to King Jonathan [
9.

lines 2ff in Col B&C are transposed
in this translation. cf p 43

42

Column A

1. הללויה מזמור ל
2. אהבת כא]
3. סרות על]
4. של יונתן המלך
5. ויראו מסנןאיך
6. רבים השמים
7. ולתהום ים]
8. ועל מפארו]
9. עני מיד צרים]
10. משכנו בציון

Column C

1. באהבתך אתים
2. על יונתן המלך
3. ובל קהל עמך
4. ישראל
5. אשר בארבע
6. רוחות שמים
7. יהי שלום כלם
8. על ממלכתך
9. יתברך שמך

Column B

1. עיר קדש
2. ביום ועד ערב מ...]
3. לקרוב להיות בן
4. פקדם לברכה...]
5. על שמך שנקרא]
6. ממלכה להברדן
7. ל ום מלחמה]
8. ליונתן המלך
9. מתן] [

PRAYER FOR
KING JONATHAN
Tefillah li-Shlomo
shel Yonatan
ha-Melekh

43

The command "And thou shalt bind them for a sign upon thy hand, and they shall be for frontlets between thine eyes" (Deut. 6:8) was practiced by Jews from early times. In the Second Temple period the sages established that *tefillin* (phylacteries; amulets in Greek) would include four scriptural passages inscribed on parchment placed in a boxlike container made of black leather. The phylacteries were worn one on the left arm and the other on the forehead. These served as a sign and a reminder that the Lord had brought the children of Israel out of Egypt (Exod. 13:9, 16).

Although the custom was known from Second Temple–period sources (*The Letter of Aristeas,* verse 159; Josephus, *Antiquities of the Jews,* IV, 213), Qumran has now provided us with the earliest remains of *tefillin,* both the leather containers and the inscribed strips of parchment. The phylactery parchments displayed here were uncovered by Pére de Vaux in Wadi Murabba'at in the Judean desert.

As a rule, phylacteries include four selections, two from Exodus (Exod. 13:1–10; 13:11–16) and two from Deuteronomy (Deut. 6:4–9; 11:13–21), that refer directly to the "sign upon thy hand" and the "frontlets between thine eyes" alluded to in the "Hear, O Israel" passage above. In this regard the Qumran phylacteries are similar to those based on the late rabbinic tradition. The scriptural verses were penned in clear minuscule characters on the elongated writing material, which was folded over to fit the minute compartments stamped into the containers.

References

Milik, J. T. "Textes Hébraux et Araméens." In *Les Grottes de Murabba'ât,* Discoveries in the Judaean Desert, II, pp. 80–85. Oxford, 1961.

Yadin, Y. "Tefillin (Phylacteries) from Qumran [XQ Phyl 1–4])" (in Hebrew), *Eretz-Israel* 9 (1969): 60–83 and plates.

3
PHYLACTERY
TEFILLIN
תפילין

Mur 4 Phyl
Copied first century–
early second century C.E.
Fragment A: 17.7 × 3 cm
(7 × 1 3/16 in.)
Fragment B: 3.8 × 2.8 cm
(1½ × 1⅛ in.)

Exod. 13:1−3

1. [1]And spoke
2. the Lord to
3. Moses
4. saying, [2]"Consecrate
5. to Me every first-born
6. the first issue of every womb of the
7. Israelites, man
8. and beast is Mine."
9. [3]And Moses said to the people,
10. "Remember this day
11. on which you went (free)
12. from Egypt, the house of bondage,
13. how with a mighty hand
14. the Lord freed you from it; no
15. leavened bread shall be eaten. [4]This day

Transcription by J. T. Milik; translation adapted from Tanakh, *pp. 103−4.*
Philadelphia, 1985.

PHYLACTERY
TEFILLIN

1. **וידבר**

2. **יהוה אל**

3. **משה**

4. **לאמר קדש**

5. **לי כל בכור פטר**

6. **כל רחם בבני**

7. **ישראל באדם**

8. **ובבהמה לי הוא**

9. **ויאמר משה אל הע͏ֿ**

10. **זכור את היום הזה**

11. **אשר יצאתם**

12. **ממצרים מבית עבדים**

13. **כי בחזק יד הוציא**

14. **יהוה אתכם מזה ולא**

15. **יאכל חמץ היום**

46

Inscribed in this scroll are parts of the final chapters (22–27) of Leviticus. It is the lowermost portion (approximately one-fifth of the original height) of the final six columns of the original manuscript. Eighteen small fragments also belong to this scroll. The additional fragments of this manuscript are from preceding chapters: Lev. 4, 10, 11, 13, 14, 16, 18–22.

The text is similar to the Masoretic text, the traditional text of the Hebrew Bible, and it proves that little change occurred over the centuries. The paleo-Hebrew script here seems to be just one manifestation of conservative traits that survived through generations and surfaced in the Hasmonean era. Hasmonean coinage of the first century B.C.E. bears similar script. Noteworthy in the scroll is the habit often observed in paleo-Hebrew script of breaking off words at the end of lines. Also characteristic is the placement of the *vav* in open spaces between paragraphs, when the new paragraph should have begun with that letter (line 2 of Hebrew transcription).

A single scribe penned the text on the grain side of the skin in an inconsistent hand, at times patient with his task, at times careless. Both vertical and horizontal lines were drawn. The vertical lines aligned the columns and margins; the horizontal lines served as guidelines from which the scribe suspended his letters. Dots were used as word spacers. This scroll was discovered in 1956, when a group of Taʻamireh Bedouin happened on Cave 11, but it was first unrolled fourteen years later, at the Israel Museum in Jerusalem.

Reference

Freedman, D. N., and K. A. Mathews. *The Paleo-Hebrew Leviticus Scroll.* Winona Lake, Indiana, 1985.

4
Leviticus
Va-Yikra
ויקרא
11Q1 (PaleoLev)
Copied late second century — early first century B.C.E.
10.9 × 100.2 cm
(4¼ × 39½ in.)

Lev. 23:22−29

1. ²²[… edges of your field, or] gather [the gleanings of your harvest; you shall leave them for the poor and the stranger: I the LO]RD [am]

2. your God.

3. ²³The LORD spoke to Moses saying: ²⁴Speak to the Israelite people thus: In the seventh month

4. on the first day of the month, you shall observe complete rest, a sacred occasion commemorated with loud blasts.

5. ²⁵You shall not work at your occupations; and you shall bring an offering by fire to the LORD.

6. ²⁶The LORD spoke to Moses saying: ²⁷Mark, the tenth day of this seventh month is the Day

7. of Atonement. It shall be a sacred occasion for you: you shall practice self-denial, and you shall bring an offering

8. by fire to the LORD; ²⁸you shall do no work throughout that day. For

9. [it is a Day of Atonement on which] expiation is made on your behalf [before the LO]RD your God. ²⁹Indeed, any person who

Translation from Tanakh, *p. 192. Philadelphia, 1985.*

1. [....] ....[רכ]....[תלקט]..... ....[תמ]..[נין].[.]יה[...]

2. ו [..]היכם.

3. ידבר.יהוה.אל.משה.לאמר.דבר.אל.בני.ישראל.לאמר.בחדש.השב

4. עי.באחד.לחדש.יהיה.לכם.שבתון.זכרון.תרועה.מקרא.קדש.ב

5. ל.מלאכת.עבדה.לא.תעשו.והקרבתמ.אשה.ליהוה.

6. וידבר.יהוה.אל.משה.לאמר.אב.בעשור.לחדש.השביעי.הזה.יומ

7. הכפרימ.הוא.מקרא.קדש.יהיה.לכם.ועניתמ.א[..]נפשתיכמ.והקרב

8. ת[..]אשה[.]ליהוה.וכל.מלאכה.לא   תעשו.בעצמ.היומ.הזה.בי.יו

9. [..... ....]ואנ[.]לכפר.עליכמ.לפנ[...]יה[..]אלהיכמ.כי.כל.הנפש.אשר

LEVITICUS
VA-YIKRA

This impressive scroll is a liturgical collection of psalms and hymns, comprising parts of forty-one biblical psalms (chiefly from chapters 101–50), in non-canonical sequence and with variations in detail. It also presents apocryphal psalms (previously unknown hymns) as well as a prose passage about the psalms composed by King David: " . . . And the total was 4,050. All these he composed through prophecy, which was given him from before the Most High" (11QPsᵃ 27:10–11).

One of the longer texts from Qumran, it was found in 1956 in Cave 11 and unrolled in 1961. Its surface is the thickest of any of the scrolls—it may be of calfskin rather than sheepskin, which was the common writing material at Qumran. The writing is on the grain side. The scroll contains twenty-eight incomplete columns of text, six of which are displayed here (cols. 14–19). Each of the preserved columns contains fourteen to eighteen lines; it is clear that six to seven lines are lacking at the bottom of each column.

The scroll's script is of fine quality, with the letters carefully drawn in the Jewish book-hand style of the Herodian period. The Tetragrammaton (the four-letter divine name) is inscribed in the paleo-Hebrew script. On paleographic grounds the manuscript is dated between 30 and 50 C.E.

Reference

Sanders, J. A. *The Psalms Scroll of Qumrân Cave 11 (11QPsᵃ)*. Discoveries in the Judaean Desert, IV. Oxford, 1965.

5
Psalms
Tehillim
תהילים
11QPs
Copied ca. 30–50 C.E.
18.5 × 86 cm
(7¼ × 33¾ in.)

Column 19: Plea for Deliverance (A Noncanonical Psalm)

1. Surely a maggot cannot praise thee nor a grave worm recount thy loving-
   kindness.
2. But the living can praise thee, even those who stumble can laud thee.
   In revealing
3. thy kindness to them and by thy righteousness thou dost enlighten them.
   For in thy hand is the soul of every
4. living thing; the breath of all flesh hast thou given. Deal with us, O
   LORD,
5. according to thy goodness, according to thy great mercy, and according
   to thy many righteous deeds. The LORD
6. has heeded the voice of those who love his name and has not deprived
   them of his loving-kindness.
7. Blessed be the LORD, who executes righteous deeds, crowning his saints
8. with loving-kindness and mercy. My soul cries out to praise thy name,
   to sing high praises
9. for thy loving deeds, to proclaim thy faithfulness—of praise of thee there
   is no end. Near death
10. was I for my sins, and my iniquities have sold me to the grave; but thou
    didst save me,
11. O LORD, according to thy great mercy, and according to thy many
    righteous deeds. Indeed have I
12. loved thy name, and in thy protection have I found refuge. When I
    remember thy might my heart
13. is brave, and upon thy mercies do I lean. Forgive my sin, O LORD,
14. and purify me from my iniquity. Vouchsafe me a spirit of faith and
    knowledge, and let me not be dishonored
15. in ruin. Let not Satan rule over me, nor an unclean spirit; neither let pain
    nor the evil
16. inclination take possession of my bones. For thou, O LORD, art my praise,
    and in thee do I hope
17. all the day. Let my brothers rejoice with me and the house of my father,
    who are astonished by the graciousness . . .
18. [   ] For e[ver] I will rejoice in thee.

Transcription and translation by J. A. Sanders

10. הייתי בחטאי ועוונותי לשאול מכרוני ותצילני

11. 𐤉𐤄𐤅𐤄 כרוב רחמיכה וכרוב צדקותיכה גם אני את

12. שמכה אהבתי ובצלכה חסיתי בזוכרי עוזכה יתקף

13. לבי ועל חסדיכה אני נסמכתי סלחה 𐤉𐤄𐤅𐤄 לחטאתי

14. וטהרני מעווני רוח אמונה ודעת חונני אל אתקלה

15. בעווה אל תשלט בי שטן ורוח טמאה מכאוב ויצר

16. רע אל ירשו בעצמי כי אתה 𐤉𐤄𐤅𐤄 שבחי ולכה קויתי

17. כול היום ישמחו אחי עמי ובית אבי השוממים בחונכה

18. [ ]לם אשמחה בכה

54

כי לוא רמה תודה לכה ולוא תספר חסדכה תולעה	1.
חי חי יודה לכה יודו לכה כול מוטטי רגל בהודיעכה	2.
חסדכה להמה וצדקתכה תשכילם כי בידכה נפש כול	3.
חי נשמת כול בשר אתה נתתה עשה עמנו יהוה	4.
כטובכה כרוב רחמיכה וכרוב צדקותיכה שמע	5.
יהוה בקול אוהבי שמו ולוא עזב חסדו מהמה	6.
ברוך יהוה עושה צדקות מעטר חסידיו	7.
חסד ורחמים שאגה נפשי להלל שמכה להודות ברנה	8.
חסדיכה להגיד אמונתכה לתהלתכה אין חקר למות	9.

Psalms
Tehillim

55

6

Hosea Commentary

Pesher Hoshe‘a

פשר הושע

4Q166 (4QpHos^a)

Copied late first

century B.C.E.

17.5 × 16.8 cm

(6⅞ × 6⅝ in.)

The text of this scroll is a commentary *(pesher)* on the biblical verses of Hosea 2:8–14. Both eschatological and historical allusions are used in interpreting the biblical text. The verse analogizes the relation of God, the husband, to Israel, the unfaithful wife. In the commentary the unfaithful ones have been led astray by "the man of the lie." The affliction befalling those led astray is famine. Although this famine could be a metaphor, it may well be a reference to an actual drought referred to in historical sources.

The manuscript shown here is the larger of two unrelated fragments of the Hosea Commentary found in Cave 4. The script, which is identical to that of a commentary on Psalms, belongs to the rustic, semiformal type of the Herodian era.

References

Allegro, J. M. *Qumrân Cave 4: I (4Q158–4Q186).* Discoveries in the Judaean Desert, V. Oxford, 1968.

Horgan, M. *Pesharim: Qumran Interpretations of Biblical Books.* Washington, 1979.

Hos. 2:10–14

1. ¹⁰[SHE DID NOT KNOW THAT] I MYSELF HAD GIVEN HER THE GRAIN
   [AND THE WINE]

2. [AND THE OIL, AND] (THAT) I HAD SUPPLIED [SILVER] AND GOLD
   {. . . .} (WHICH) THEY MADE [INTO BAAL. The interpretation of it is]

3. that [they] ate [and] were satisfied, and they forgot God who [had fed
   them, and all]

4. his commandments they cast behind them, which he had sent to them
   [by]

5. his servants the prophets. But to those who led them astray they listened,
   and they honored them [   ]

6. and as if they were gods, they fear them in their blindness.

7. *vacat*

8. ¹¹THEREFORE, I SHALL TAKE BACK MY GRAIN AGAIN IN ITS TIME AND
   MY WINE [IN ITS SEASON,]

9. AND I SHALL WITHDRAW MY WOOL AND MY FLAX FROM COVERING
   [HER NAKEDNESS.]

10. ¹²I SHALL NOW UNCOVER HER PRIVATE PARTS IN THE SIGHT OF [HER]
    LO[VERS AND]

11. NO [ONE] WILL WITHDRAW HER FROM MY HAND.

12. The interpretation of it is that he smote them with famine and with
    nakedness so that they became a disgra[ce]

13. and a reproach in the sight of the nations on whom they had leaned for
    support, but they

14. will not save them from their afflictions. ¹³AND I SHALL PUT AN END TO
    ALL HER JOY,

15. [HER] PIL[GRIMAGE,] HER [NEW] MOON, AND HER SABBATH, AND ALL
    HER FEASTS. The interpretation of it is that

16. they make [the fe]asts go according to the appointed times of the nation.
    And [all]

17. [joy] has been turned for them into mourning.
    ¹⁴AND I SHALL MAKE DESOLATE [HER VINE]

18. [AND HER FIG TREE,] OF WHICH SHE SAID, "THEY ARE THE HIRE
    [THAT MY LOVERS HAVE GIVEN] ME."

19. AND I SHALL MAKE THEM A FOREST, AND THE W[ILD BEAST OF THE
    FIELD] WILL DEVOUR THEM.

Transcription and translation by M. Horgan

HOSEA COMMENTARY
PESHER HOSHEʿA

1. ‏[לוא ידעה כיא] אנוכי נתתי לה הדגן [והתירוש]
2. ‏[והיצהר וכסף] הרביתי וזהב ... עשו [לבעל פשרו]
3. ‏אשר [אכלו וי]שבעו וישכחו את כל המ[נאכלם ואת כול]
4. ‏מצוותיו השליכו אחרי גום אשר שלח אליהם [ביד]
5. ‏עבדיו הנביאים ולמתעיהם שמעו ויכבדום [ ]
6. ‏וכאלים יפחדו מהם בעורונם [ ]
7. *vacat*
8. ‏לכן אשוב ולקחתי דגני בעתו ותירושי [במועדו]
9. ‏והצלתי צמרי ופישתי מלכסות את [ערותה]
10. ‏ועתה אגלה את נבלותה לעיני מאה[ביה ואיש]
11. ‏לוא יצילנה מידי
12. ‏פשרו אשר הכם ברעב ובערום להיות לקלו[ן]
13. ‏וחרפה לעיני הגואים אשר נשענו עליהם והמה
14. ‏לוא יושיעום מצרותיהם והשבתי כול משושה
15. ‏ח[ו]גה חד[ש]ה ושבתה וכול מועדיה פשרו אשר
16. ‏[את המו]עדות יוליכו במועדי הגואים ו[כול]
17. ‏[שמחה] נהפכה להם לאבל והשמותי [גפנה]
18. ‏[ותאנתה] אשר אמרה אתנם הם לי [אשר נתנו]
19. ‏[לי מאהב]י ושמתים ליער ואכלתם ח[ית השדה]

58

7
COMMUNITY RULE
SEREKH HA-YAḤAD
סרך היחד
4Q258 (S^d)
Copied late first
century B.C.E.–
early first century C.E.
8.8 × 21.5 cm
(3⁷⁄16 × 8⁷⁄16 in.)

Originally known as the Manual of Discipline, the Community Rule *(Serekh ha-Yaḥad)* contains regulations ordering the life of the members of the *yaḥad,* the group within the Judean Desert sect who chose to live communally. The strict rules of conduct they adopted for themselves formed the basis for the observance of the commandments of the Torah as the will of God. These commandments, however, are not cited in this scroll. The rules of conduct, which are accompanied by admonitions and punishments to be imposed on violators, deal with the manner of joining the group, the relations between the members, their way of life, and their beliefs. The sect divided humanity between the righteous and the wicked and asserted that human nature and everything that happens in the world are irrevocably predestined. The scroll ends with songs of praise to God.

A complete copy of the scroll, eleven columns in length, was found in Cave 1. Ten fragmentary copies were recovered in Cave 4, and a small section was found in Cave 5. The large number of manuscripts attests to the importance of this text for the sect. The manuscript shown here is the longest of the versions of this text found in Cave 4; it differs from the Cave 1 manuscript in that it is formulated in a more concise fashion.

Paleographic study of the Community Rule scroll indicates that it is in Herodian bookhand, whereas the complete scroll from Cave 1 is probably from the earlier part of the Hasmonean period.

Reference

Qimron, E. "A Preliminary Publication of 4QS^d Columns VII–VIII" (in Hebrew). *Tarbiz* 60 (1991): 435–37.

And according to his insight he shall admit him. In this way both his love and his hatred. No man shall argue or quarrel with the men of perdition. He shall keep his council in secrecy in the midst of the men of deceit and admonish with knowledge, truth and righteous commandment those of chosen conduct, each according to his spiritual quality and according to the norm of time. He shall guide them with knowledge and instruct them in the mysteries of wonder and truth in the midst of the members of the community, so that they shall behave decently with one another in all that has been revealed to them. That is the time for studying the Torah (lit. clearing the way) in the wilderness. He shall instruct them to do all that is required at that time, and to separate from all those who have not turned aside from all deceit.

These are the norms of conduct for the Master in those times with respect to his loving and to his everlasting hating of the men of perdition in a spirit of secrecy. He shall leave to them property and wealth and earnings like a slave to his lord, (showing) humility before the one who rules over him. He shall be zealous concerning the Law and be prepared for the Day of Revenge.

He shall perform the will [of God] in all his deeds and in all strength as He has commanded. He shall freely delight in all that befalls him, and shall desire nothing except God's will. . . .

Transcription and translation by E. Qimron

1. ולפי שכלו להגישו וכן אהבתו עם שנאתו ואשר לא יוכיח איש ולא
   יתרובב עם אנשי ה(דע)[שח]ת

2. ולסתר עצתו בתוך אנשי העול ולהוכיח דעת אמת ומשפט צדק
   לבחירי דרך איש כרוחו וכתכון

3. העת ל[הנחות]ם בדעה וכן להשכילם ברזי פלא ואמת בתוך אנשי
   היחד להלך תמים איש את

4. [רעהו בכל] הנגלה להם היא עת פנות הדרך למדבר [ו]להשכילם
   בכל הנמצא לעשות בעת

5. [הזאת והבדל] מכל איש אשר לא הסיר דרכו מכול עול   ואלה
   תכוני הדרך למשכיל בעת[ים]

6. [האלה לאהבתו עם] שנאתו שנאת עולם עם אנשי השחת ברוח
   הסתר ולעזוב למו הון ובצע

7. [ועמל כעבד למוש]ל בו וענוה לפני הרודה בו ולהיות איש מקנא
   לחוק ועתי ליום נקם לע[שות]

8. [רצון בכל משלח כפים ובכ]ל ממשלו כאש[ר צוה וכ]ל הנעשה בו
   ירצה בנדבה וזולת רצון [אל]

COMMUNITY RULE
SEREKH HA-YAḤAD

63

8
SOME TORAH
PRECEPTS
MIQṢAT MAʿASE
HA-TORAH
מקצת מעשי התורה
4Q396 (MMT^c)
Copied late first
century B.C.E.—
early first century C.E.
Fragment A: 8 × 12.9 cm
(3⅛ × 5 in.)
Fragment B: 4.3 × 7 cm
(1 11/16 × 2¾ in.)
Fragment C: 9.1 ×
17.4 cm (3 9/16 × 6⅞ in.)

This scroll is a sectarian polemical document, of which six incomplete manuscripts have been discovered. Together, these fragments provide a composite text of about 130 lines, which probably cover two-thirds of the original. The initial part of the text is completely lacking. The scroll is commonly referred to as MMT, an abbreviation of its Hebrew name, *Miqṣat Maʿase ha-Torah,* which appears in the epilogue.

The document, apparently in letter form, is unique in language, style, and content. Using linguistic and theological considerations, the original text has been dated as one of the earliest works of the Qumran sect.

Apparently it consisted of four sections: (1) the opening formula, now lost; (2) a calendar of 364 days; (3) a list of more than twenty rulings in religious law *(Halakhot),* most of which are peculiar to the sect; and (4) an epilogue that deals with the separation of the sect from the multitude of the people and attempts to persuade the addressee to adopt the sect's legal views. The *Halakhot* are the core of the letter; the remainder of the text is merely the framework. The calendar, although a separate section, was probably also related to the sphere of *Halakhah.* These *Halakhot* deal chiefly with the Temple and its ritual. The author states that disagreement on these matters caused the sect to secede from Israel.

Because the beginning of the text is lost, the identities of both the author and the addressee are missing. However, a commentary *(pesher)* to Psalm 37 relates that the "teacher of righteousness" conveyed a letter to his opponent, the "wicked priest." This may well be a reference to this document, which is addressed to "the leader of Israel."

In general, the script belongs to the semiformal tradition of Herodian times. It is noteworthy that several letters, formal and semiformal, exhibit early and late typological forms at the same time. The majority of the manuscripts are inscribed on parchment, although several papyrus fragments also have survived.

References

Strugnell, J., and E. Qimron. Discoveries in the Judaean Desert, X. Oxford, forthcoming.

Sussmann, Y. "The History of *Halakha* and the Dead Sea Scrolls—Preliminary Observations on Miqsat Maʿase Ha-Torah (4QMMT)" (in Hebrew), *Tarbiz* 59 (1990): 11–76.

1. until sunset on the eighth day. And concerning [the impurity] of
2. the [dead] person we are of the opinion that every bone, whether it
3. has its flesh on it or not—should be (treated) according to the law of the dead or the slain.
4. And concerning the mixed marriages that are being performed among the people, and they are sons of holy [seed],
5. as is written, Israel is holy. And concerning his (Israel's) [clean] animal
6. it is written that one must not let it mate with another species, and concerning his clothes [it is written that they should not]
7. be of mixed stuff; and one must not sow his field and vineyard with mixed species.
8. Because they (Israel) are holy, and the sons of Aaron are [most holy.]
9. But you know that some of the priests and [the laity intermingle]
10. [And they] adhere to each other and pollute the holy seed
11. as well as their (i.e., the priests') own [seed] with corrupt women. Since [the sons of Aaron should . . .]

Transcription and translation by J. Strugnell and E. Qimron

1. עד בוא השמש ביום השמיני ועל [טמאת נפש]

2. האדם אנחנו אומרים שכול עצם ש[הוא חסרה]

3. ושלמה כמשפט המת או החלל הוא *vacat*

4. ועל הזונות הנעסה בתוך העם והמה ב[ני זרע]

5. קדש משכתוב קודש ישראל ועל בה[מתו הטהורה]

6. כתוב שלוא לרבעה כלאים ועל לבושו כתוב שלוא]

7. יהיה שעטנז ושלוא לזרוע שדו וכ[רמו כלאים]

8. [ב]גלל שהמה קדושים ובני אהרון ק[דושי קדושים]

9. [וא]תם יודעים שמקצת הכהנים וה[עם מתערבים]

10. [והם] מתוככים ומטמאי[ם] את זרע [הקודש ואף]

11. את [זרע]ם עם הזונות כ[י לבני אהרון   ]

The Songs of the Sabbath Sacrifice, also known as the Angelic Liturgy, is a liturgical work composed of thirteen sections, one for each of the first thirteen Sabbaths of the year. The songs evoke angelic praise and elaborate on angelic priesthood, the heavenly temple, and the Sabbath worship in that temple.

The headings of the various songs reflect the solar calendar of the Qumran sect. Although the songs bear no explicit indication of their source, the phraseology and terminology of the texts are similar to those of other Qumran works. It appears, therefore, that the Songs of the Sabbath Sacrifice is a sectarian work.

Eight manuscripts of this work were found in Qumran Cave 4 (4Q400 through 407) and one in Cave 11, dating from the late Hasmonean and Herodian periods. One manuscript of the Songs of the Sabbath Sacrifice was found at Masada, perhaps reflecting a sectarian presence or influence in the Zealot fortress.

References

Newsom, C. *Songs of the Sabbath Sacrifice: A Critical Edition*. Atlanta, 1985.
Strugnell, J. "The Angelic Liturgy at Qumrân—4Q Serek Širôt ʿOlat Haššabbât." In *Congress Volume, Oxford 1959. Supplements to Vetus Testamentum*, vol. 7, pp. 318–45. Leiden, 1960.

9
SONGS OF THE
SABBATH SACRIFICE
SHIROT ʿOLAT
HA-SHABBAT
שירות עולת השבת
4Q403 (ShirShabb^d)
*Copied mid-first
century B.C.E.*
*18 × 19 cm
(7 × 7½ in.)*

30. By the instructor. Song of the sacrifice of the seventh Sabbath on the sixteenth of the month. Praise the God of the lofty heights, O you lofty ones among all the

31. *elim* of knowledge. Let the holiest of the godlike ones sanctify the King of glory who sanctifies by holiness all His holy ones. O you chiefs of the praises of

32. all the godlike beings, praise the splendidly [pr]aiseworthy God. For in the splendor of praise is the glory of His realm. From it (comes) the praises of all

33. the godlike ones together with the splendor of all [His] maj[esty. And] exalt his exaltedness to exalted heaven, you most godlike ones of the lofty *elim,* and (exalt) His glorious divinity above

34. all the lofty heights. For H[e is God of gods] of all the chiefs of the heights of heaven and King of ki[ngs] of all the eternal councils. (by the intention of)

35. (His knowledge) At the words of His mouth come into being [all the lofty angels]; at the utterance of His lips all the eternal spirits; [by the in]tention of His knowledge all His creatures

36. in their undertakings. Sing with joy, you who rejoice [in His knowledge with] rejoicing among the wondrous godlike beings. And chant His glory with the tongue of all who chant with knowledge; and (chant) His wonderful songs of joy

37. with the mouth of all who chant [of Him. For He is] God of all who rejoice {in knowledge} forever and Judge in His power of all the spirits of understanding.

Transcription and translation by C. Newsom

30. למשכיל שיר עולת השבת השביעית בשש עשר לחודש הללו
אלוהי מרומים הרמים בכול

31. אלי דעת יקדילו קדושי אלוהים למלך הכבוד המקדיש בקודעו
לכול קדושו ראשי תושבחות

32. כול אלוהים שבחו לאלוהי ת[אלוה]י ת[ת]שבחות הוד כי בהדר תשבחות כבוד
מלכותו בה תשבחות כול

33. אלוהים עם הדר כול מלכ[ו]תו ו[רו]ממו רוממו למרום אלוהים
מאלי רום ואלוהות כבודו מעל

Songs of the
Sabbath Sacrifice
Shirot 'Olat
ha-Shabbat

34. לכול מרומי רום כיא הו[א] אל אלים] לכול ראשי מרומים
ומלך מלכ[ים] לכל סודי עולמים ברצון

35. דעת לאמרי פיהו יהיו כ[ול אלי רום] למוצא שפתיו כול
רוחי עולמים [בר]צון דעתו כול מעשיו

36. במשלחם רננו מרנני [דעתו ב]רונן באלוהי פלא והגו
כבודו בלשון כול הוגי דעת רנות פלאו

37. בפי כול הוגי [בו כיא הוא] אלוהים לכול מרנני דעת עד
ושופט בגבורתו לכול רוחי בין

Among the numerous fragments of calendrical documents from Qumran, some, like this one from Cave 4, have distinctive features. Two special nights in every month of the lunar calendar of 354 days, which the wider Jewish community embraced, are listed in order, in a cycle of six years, that is, over seventy-two months: the night following that of the full moon in the middle of the month, when the moon begins to wane, and the night of the moon's total eclipse at the end of the month. While the first of these nights bears no specific designation, the other is denoted *duqah* or *duqo(h),* a term for the moon's thinness.

The dark, and therefore ominous, nights are dated by attaching them to days that precede them in the solar cycle of 364 days to which the Qumran community adhered. At the same time they are also synchronized with the concurrent days of the week of service in the Jerusalem Temple of a specific priestly watch.

It appears that these rosters, penned in a late Hasmonean or early Herodian bookhand, were intended to provide the members of the New Covenant with a timetable for abstaining from important activities on the days before the dark phases of the moon's waning and eclipse. In contrast, rabbinic tradition puts a premium on the moon's bright phases: the night of the new moon at the beginning of the month and the night of the full moon in its middle.

References

Jaubert, A. "Le Calendrier de Jubilés et de la Secte de Qumrân: Ses origines Bibliques," *Vetus Testamentum* 3 (1953): 250–64.

Talmon, S. "The Calendar of the Judean Covenanteers." In *The World of Qumran from Within: Collected Studies,* pp. 147–85. Jerusalem, 1989.

Talmon, S., and I. Knohl. "A Calendrical Scroll from Qumran Cave IV—Miš Ba (4Q321)" (in Hebrew), *Tarbiz* 60 (1991): 505–21.

10

CALENDRICAL
DOCUMENT
MISHMAROT
משמרות

4Q321 (Mishmarot Bᵃ)
Copied ca. 50–25 B.C.E.
13.4 × 21.1 cm
(5¼ × 8¼ in.)

1. [on the first {day} in {the week of} Jedaiah {which falls} on the tw]elfth in it {the seventh month}. On the second {day} in {the week of} Abia[h {which falls} on the twenty-f[ifth in the eighth {month}; and *duqah* {is} on the third] {day}

2. [in {the week of} Miyamin {which falls} on the twelfth] in it {the eighth month}. On the third {day} in {the week of} Jaqim {which falls} on the twen[ty-fourth in the ninth {month}; and *duqah* {is} on the fourth] {day}

3. [in {the week of} Shekaniah {which falls} on the eleven]th in it {the ninth month}. On the fifth {day} in {the week of} Immer {which falls} on the twe[n]ty-third in the te[nth {month}; and *duqah* {is} on the sixth {day} in {the week of Je]shbeab {which falls}

4. [on the tenth in] it {the tenth month}. On the [si]xth {day} in {the week of} Jeḥezkel {which falls} on the twenty-second in the eleventh month [and *duqah* {is on the} Sabbath in] {the week of} Petaḥah {which falls}

5. [on the ninth in it {the eleventh month}]. On the first {day} in {the week of} Joiarib {which falls} on the t[w]enty-second in the twelfth month; and [*duqah* {is} on the seco]nd {day}] in {the week of} Delaiah {which falls}

6. [on the ninth in it] {the twelfth month}. *vacat* The] se[cond] {year}: The first {month}. On the sec[on]d {day} in {the week of} Malakiah {which falls} on the tw[entieth in it {the first month}; and] *duqah* {is}

7. [on the third {day} in {the week of} Harim {which falls} on the seventh] in it {the first month}. On the fou[r]th {day} in {the week of} Jeshua {which falls} [on] the twentieth in the second {month}; and [*duqah* {is} on the fifth {day} in {the week of]} Haqqoṣ {which falls} on the seventh

8. [in it {the second month}. On the fifth {day} in {the week of} Ḥuppah {which falls} on the nine]teenth in the third {month}; and *duqa*[h] {is} on the six[th {day} in {the week of} Happisses {which falls}

Translation and transcription by S. Talmon and I. Knohl

1. ‏[באחד בידעיה בשני]ם עשר בוא בשנים באבי[ה בחמישה]‏
‏ועש[רים בשמיני ודוקה בשלושה]‏

2. ‏[במימין בשנים עשר] בוא בשלושה ביקים בא[ר]בעה ועשרים‏
‏בתשיעי ודוקה בארבעה]‏

3. ‏[בשכניה בעשתי ע]שר בוא בחמשה באמר בשלושה וע[ש]רים‏
‏בעש[י]רי ודוקה בששה בי[ן]שבאב‏

4. ‏[בעשרה בו]א ב[ש]שה ביחזקאל בשנים ועשרים בעשתי עשר‏
‏החודש ו[ד]וקה שבת ב[פ]תחה‏

5. ‏[בתשעה בוא] באחד ביויריב בשנ[י]ם ועשרים בשנים עשר החודש‏
‏ו[ד]וקה בשנ[י]ם בדליה‏

6. ‏[בתשעה בוא *vacat* השנה ה[שנ]ית] הראשון בשנ[י]ם במלאכה‏
‏בע[ש]רים בוא ו[ד]וקה‏

7. ‏[בשלושה בחרים בשבעה] בוא בארב[ע]ה בישוע [ב]עשרים בשני‏
‏ו[ד]וקה בחמשה ב[ק]וץ בשבעה‏

8. ‏[בוא בחמשה בחופה בתשעה] עשר בשלישי ודוק[ה] בשש[ה]‏
‏בא[ל]ישי[ב ב]ש[ו]שה [בוא שב]ת בפצץ‏

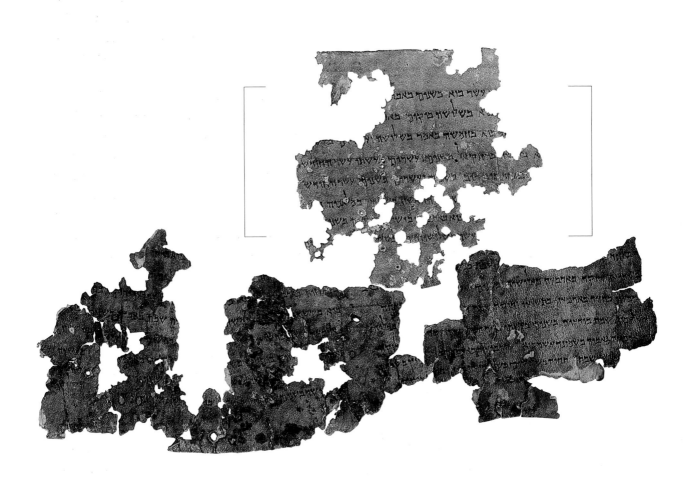

One of the most important apocryphic works of the Second Temple period is Enoch. According to the biblical narrative (Gen. 5:21–24), Enoch lived 365 years (far less than the other antediluvian patriarchs) and "walked with God; then he was no more for God took him."

Rabbinic sources and pseudepigraphic literature attach many tales and legends to this figure. He is all wise, knowing the secrets of the universe and being the source of information for natural and supernatural occurrences. The fullest portrait of Enoch emerges in 1 Enoch, a work preserved in its entirety only in Geʿez (Old Ethiopic).

The Book of Enoch is the earliest of the pseudepigraphic books. It is quoted in Jubilees and the Testaments of the Twelve Patriarchs, is referred to in the New Testament (Jude 1:14), and was used by the author of the Damascus Document.

The original language of most of this work was, in all likelihood, Aramaic, which was lost in antiquity. Portions of a Greek translation were discovered in Egypt, and quotations were known from the church fathers. The discovery of the texts from Qumran Cave 4 has finally provided parts of the Aramaic original, covering 1 Enoch. The Qumran text includes the Book of Giants, previously known from Manichaean adaptations in a variety of languages.

The Qumran manuscripts of Enoch have been dated paleographically from the early second century to the end of the first century B.C.E. The two texts presented here are from 4QEnᵃ, which is attributed to the first half of the second century B.C.E.

In the fragment exhibited, humankind is called on to observe how unchanging nature follows God's will. In the first verse transcribed here, man is chastised for changing His work and transgressing. Further along, it states that humankind will be cursed for eternity. In the second verse, the Watchers saw the beautiful daughters of humankind and desired them for wives. They are bound together by oath, and the names of the twenty Chiefs of Ten, known from later tradition, are given. The lines presented here (13–16) tell about their taking wives and teaching them occult arts. The wives gave birth to giants, who wreak destruction.

II
ENOCH
ḤANOKH
חנוך

4Q201 (En arᵃ)
Copied ca. 200–150 B.C.E
Fragment A: 17.5 × 17.5 cm (6⅞ × 6⅞ in.)
Fragment B: 6.4 × 6.9 cm (2½ × 2¹¹⁄₁₆ in.)

Reference

Milik, J. T. *The Books of Enoch: Aramaic Fragments of Qumran Cave 4.* Oxford, 1976.

Enᵃ I ii

12. ... But you have changed your works,

13. [and have not done according to his command, and tran]sgressed against him; (and have spoken) haughty and harsh words, with your impure mouths,

14. [against his majesty, for your heart is hard]. You will have no peace.

Enᵃ I iii

13. [They (the leaders) and all ... of them took for themselves]

14. wives from all that they chose and [they began to cohabit with them and to defile themselves with them];

15. and to teach them sorcery and [spells and the cutting of roots; and to acquaint them with herbs.]

16. And they become pregnant by them and bo[re (great) giants three thousand cubits high ...]

Transcription by J. T. Milik, amended by J. C. Greenfield;
translation by J. C. Greenfield

12. ‏...ואנתן שניתן עבדכן

13. ‏[ולא תעבדון ממרה ותע]ברון עלוהי [ותמללון] רברבן וקשין
בפום (!) טמתכן

14. ‏[על רבותה די קשה לבב]כן לת שלם לכן...

ENOCH

ḤANOKH

13. ‏[אנון ו...בלהן נסבו להן]

14. ‏נשין מן כל די בחרו ו[שריו למנעל עליהן ולאסתאבה בהן]

15. ‏ולאלפה אנין חרשה ו[כשפה ומקטע שרשין ולאחויה להן עסבין]

16. ‏והויה בטנן מנהן ויל[דן גברין רמין תלתת אלפין אמה...]

12
WAR RULE
SEREKH
HA-MILḤAMAH
סרך המלחמה
4Q285 (SM)
Copied early first
century C.E.
4 × 5 cm (1½ × 2 in.)

This six-line fragment, written in a Herodian script of the first half of the first century C.E., refers to a Messiah from the Branch of David, to a judgment, and to a killing. The word **והמיתו** (line 4) could suggest "and the Prince of the Congregation, the Branch of David, will kill him," but the nonvocalized reading also allows for "and they killed the Prince." The text was therefore dubbed the "Pierced Messiah" text. The transcription and translation presented here support the "killing Messiah" interpretation, alluding to a triumphant Messiah (Is. 11:4).

References

Tabor, J. "A Pierced or Piercing Messiah?—The Verdict Is Still Out," *Biblical Archaeology Review* 18 (1992): 58–59.

Vermes, G. "The Oxford Forum for Qumran Research: Seminar on the Rule of War from Cave 4 (4Q285)," *Journal of Jewish Studies* 43 (Spring 1992): 85–90.

1.]Isaiah the prophet: [The thickets of the forest] will be cut [down
2. with an axe and Lebanon by a majestic one will f]all. And there shall
    come forth a shoot from the stump of Jesse [
3.]the Branch of David and they will enter into judgement with [
4.]and the Prince of the Congregation, the Bran[ch of David] will kill him
    [
5. by stroke]s and by wounds. And a Priest [of renown (?)] will command [
6. the s]lai[n] of the Kitti[m]

Transcription and translation by G. Vermes

WAR RULE
SEREKH
HA-MILḤAMAH

1.]ישעיהו הנביא ונוק[פו

2. י]פול ויצא חוטר מגזע ישי [

3.]צמח דויד ונשפטו את [

4.]והמיתו נשיא העדה צמ[ח דויד

5.]גם ובמחוללות וצוה כוהן [

6. ח]ללו[ן כתיים [   ]ל[

FROM THE
QUMRAN RUIN

In the 1955 season of excavations at Qumran, three intact ceramic vessels containing 561 silver coins were found under a doorway between Levels Ib and II. The vessels were filled to the brim with coins, and the mouth of one of the vessels was covered with a palm-fiber stopper.

Pére Roland de Vaux, excavator of Qumran, relied heavily on the coin evidence for his dating and interpretations of the various phases of the site. The early coins in the hoard were tetradrachms of Antiochus VII Sidetes and Demetrius II Nicator (136/135 to 127/126 B.C.E.), minted in Tyre, as well as six Roman Republican coins from the mid-first century B.C.E. The bulk of the hoard represents the autonomous continuation of the Seleucid mint: the well-known series of Tyrian *shekalim* and half-*shekalim*, minted from 126/125 B.C.E. onward. These are the same coins that were prescribed in the Temple for the poll tax and other payments (Tosefta. *Ketubot* 13, 20).

Two of the three hoard vessels are of a type otherwise unknown in the ceramic repertoire at Qumran. De Vaux suggested that this fact corroborated the information in the Community Rule, which relates that new adherents in the sect were to surrender their worldly goods to the treasurer of the community. The vessels and their contents would then constitute the deposit of one or a number of new adherents. On the other hand, it should be noted that foundation deposits of coins — often under doorways — were common in antiquity.

Shown here are twenty-four Tyrian *shekalim* and half-*shekalim* minted between the years 103/102 and 10/9 B.C.E.

Donald T. Ariel

References

Meshorer, Y. *Ancient Jewish Coinage.* Dix Hills, N.Y., 1982.

Sharabani, M. "Monnaies de Qumrân au Musée Rockefeller de Jérusalem," *Revue Biblique* 87 (1980): 274–84.

13

HOARD OF COINS
24 silver coins
136/135 B.C.E.–10/9 B.C.E.
Diameter 1.9–2.8 cm
(¾–1⅛ in.)

The obverse shows the diademed head of Demetrius to the right. On the reverse is an eagle perched on a prow, at its shoulder a palm branch; in the left field is a club surmounted by the monogram of Tyre and the letters ΑΡΕ; in the right field are the letters ΑΞ and the date ϜΠΡ (186 of the Seleucid era); between the eagle's legs is the symbol ⊨. Around all is the inscription ΒΑΣΙΛΕΩΣ ΔΗΜΗΤΡΙΟΥ (Of King Demetrius).

On the obverse of this coin is a laureate head of Melqarth (in his Hellenized form as Heracles) to the right. The reverse shows an eagle on a prow, a palm branch at its shoulder; in the left field is a club and the date ϘΘ (99 of the Tyrian era); in the right field is a monogram Ⰰ; between the eagle's legs is the symbol ꝯ. The inscription ΤΥΡΟΥ ΙΕΡΑΣ ΚΑΙ ΑΣΥΛΟΥ (Of holy, sanctuary-providing Tyre) encircles the coin.

13A
TETRADRACHM
OF DEMETRIUS II
Q65
127/126 B.C.E.
Diameter 2.7 cm (1 in.)

13B
TYRIAN SHEKEL
Q3
28/27 B.C.E.
Diameter 2.7 cm (1 in.)

Pottery, coins, and written material found at an archeological site allow for the establishment of a relative and an absolute chronological and cultural framework. Consequently, the pottery found in the Dead Sea area disclosed many facets of the Qumran story.

The vessels shown here are representative of the finds from the immediate area of Qumran. Items from the surrounding caves and openings in the cliffs proved to be identical to those excavated at the Qumran site itself. It seems to have been a regional center—most likely a single pottery workshop supplied the entire area.

The repertory of ceramic finds from Qumran is limited and, apart from a large number of cylindrical scroll jars, consists chiefly of modest items of daily use: juglets, flasks, drinking cups, cooking pots, serving dishes, and bowls. A storeroom found during the excavation contained more than a thousand pottery items arranged by usage: vessels for cooking, serving, pouring, drinking, and dining.

References

De Vaux, R. *Archaeology and the Dead Sea Scrolls.* London, 1973.

Lapp, P. *Palestinian Ceramic Chronology, 200 B.C.–A.D. 70.* New Haven, 1961.

Some of the Dead Sea Scrolls were found by Bedouin shepherds in 1947 in cylindrical pottery jars of this type, which are unknown elsewhere. The discovery of these singular vessels in the Qumran excavations as well as in the caves, where they held scrolls, is considered by many to be convincing evidence of the link between the settlement and the caves. These jars, as well as the other pottery vessels recovered at Qumran, are probably of local manufacture.

14
JAR WITH LID
Pottery
KhQ 1474
First century B.C.E.–
first century C.E.
Lid: Height 5 cm (2 in.),
diameter 17.8 cm (7 in.).
Jar: Height 49.8 cm
(19½ in.), diameter
24 cm (9⅜ in.)

15

HERODIAN LAMP
Pottery with fiber wick
52.2
First century B.C.E.–
first century C.E.
Height 4.3 cm (1¹¹⁄₁₆
in.), length 10 cm
(4 in.)

The earliest occurrences of this type of lamp were in strata associated with Herod's reign (37–4 B.C.E.). However, the dating of the lamp has been modified by recent excavations. A similar lamp type was uncovered in the Jewish Quarter of Jerusalem, in strata relating to the destruction of the Second Temple (70 C.E.), thus indicating a date later than was previously assumed.

The lamp's characteristic features are a circular wheel-made body, flat unmarked base, and large central filling hole. The spatulate nozzle was separately handformed and subsequently attached to the body. Traces of a palm-fiber wick were found in the lamp's nozzle.

Two inkwells were found at the Qumran excavations, this one of pottery and another of bronze. They were in the vicinity of a large table, which suggested to the site's excavators scribal activity in a scriptorium. It is feasible that many of the manuscripts were written or copied locally, although manuscripts of earlier date and other locations may well occur.

This cylindrical pottery vessel has a flat base and a small, circular, rimmed opening at the top for dipping the pen and topping up the ink. This type of vessel also was found in excavations in Jerusalem.

16
Inkwell
Pottery
I.2179
Late first century B.C.E.–
early first century C.E.
Height 4.6 cm (1¾ in.),
diameter 3.9 cm (1½ in.)

17
PLATES
Pottery
KhQ 1591 a–o
First century B.C.E.–
first century C.E.
Height 2.6–5.5 cm
(1–2³⁄₁₆ in.),
diameter 13.6–16.4 cm
(13⅜–6⁷⁄₁₆ in.)

Plates, bowls, and goblets were found in one of the rooms at Qumran, with dozens of vessels piled one on top of the other. This room probably served as a crockery (a storage space) near the assembly room, which may have served as a dining room.

The wheel-made plates are shallow, with a ring base and upright rim. The firing is metallic. Hundreds of plates were recovered, most of them complete, some with traces of soot.

18

Two-Handled Jar
Pottery
KhQ 1634
First century B.C.E.–
first century C.E.
Height 37.25 cm
(14½ in.), diameter
18.7 cm (7¼ in.)

This elongated, barrel-shaped jar has a ring base, a ribbed body, a very short wide neck, and two loop handles. The vessel was probably used to store provisions.

An elongated piece with a ribbed body and a ring base, this vase has a short neck that is turned inside out.

19
VASE
Pottery
KhQ 364
First century B.C.E.–
first century C.E.
Height 17 cm (6⅝ in.),
diameter 9.5 cm
(3¾ in.)

20

JUG

Pottery

KhQ 1192

First century B.C.E.–
first century C.E.

*Height 19.5 cm (7⅝ in.),
diameter 14 cm (5½ in.)*

This globular jug has a ribbed body and a long, tapering neck ending in a splayed rim. A single-loop handle extends from the rim to the upper part of the body.

This flattened pot has a ribbed shoulder and a short, wide neck. The firing is metallic.

21
COOKING POT
Pottery
KhQ 1565
First century B.C.E.–
first century C.E.
Height 15 cm (5⅞ in.),
diameter 24 cm (9⅜ in.)

22

COOKING POT

Pottery

KhQ 2506

First century B.C.E.–
first century C.E.

Height 20.5 cm (8 in.),
diameter 26 cm (10¼ in.)

A globular-shaped design, this pot is similar to item no. 23 opposite. The surface of the body, from shoulder to base, is ribbed. Two ribbed handles span the vessel from the rim to the upper part of the shoulder. The firing is metallic. Traces of soot are discernible over the lower part.

23
COOKING POT
Pottery
KhQ 2506/a
First century B.C.E.–
first century C.E.
Height 22 cm (8⅝ in.),
diameter 23 cm (9 in.)

24

Bowls

Pottery

KhQ 1601/a

First century B.C.E.–
first century C.E.

Bowl A: Height 8.5 cm
(3⅜ in.), diameter
12.4 cm (4⅞ in.)

Bowl B: Height 9.2 cm
(3⅝ in.), diameter
13.5 cm (5⁵⁄₁₆ in.)

Hemispherical in shape, these bowls have a ring base and an inverted rim.

25

Goblets

Pottery (stacked)

KhQ 1587 a–h

First century B.C.E.–
first century C.E.

Height 26.5 cm
(10⁷⁄₁₆ in.), diameter
16 cm (6¼ in.)

Found in a stack, these identical V-shaped drinking goblets are of fine ware. They were found in the pottery storeroom, excavated in the Qumran ruin.

Stone vessels, usually manufactured of easily workable, soft limestone, were commonly found in the Jerusalem area in the late Second Temple period. They were abundant in Qumran in a variety of shapes and sizes and demonstrate expert workmanship.

The reason for their existence can be found in Jewish ritual law *(Halakhah)*. Stone—as opposed to pottery—does not become ritually unclean *(tamei)*. Jewish law maintains that pottery vessels that have become ritually unclean must be broken, never to be used again, whereas in similar circumstances stone vessels retain their ritual purity and need not be discarded (Mishnah. *Kelim* 10:11; *Parah* 3:2).

Widespread use of these stone vessels is particularly evident because of their discovery in the excavations of the Jewish Quarter in Jerusalem. Some of these vessels served the same functions as ceramic vessels, and some had particular shapes and functions. Although the raw material is common in Jerusalem, the cost of production was, no doubt, far greater than that of pottery. The flourishing manufacture of stone vessels came to an end in the wake of the destruction of the Second Temple (70 C.E.).

This large goblet-shaped vessel was produced on a lathe, probably in Jerusalem, and shows excellent craftsmanship. It is surprising that an ancient lathe was capable of supporting and working such a large and heavy stone block. The vessel may shed light on the shape of the *kallal* mentioned in the Talmudic sources— the vessel holding the purification ashes of the red heifer (Mishnah. *Parah* 3:3).

STONE VESSELS

26
LARGE GOBLET
Limestone
First century C.E.
Height 72 cm (28¼ in.),
diameter 38.5 cm
(15⅛ in.)

27
MEASURING CUPS
Limestone
KhQ 1036, KhQ 1604
First century C.E.
Cup A: Height 7.5 cm
(3 in.), diameter 8 cm
(3⅛ in.)
Cup B: Height 12.8 cm
(5 in.), diameter 19.4 cm
(7½ in.)

Cylindrical cups of this type, ranging in height between 5 and 15 centimeters, are frequently found in sites of the Second Temple period. It is believed that their capacities correspond to the dry and liquid measures mentioned in the Mishnah.

These vessels were pared with a knife or adze, and their surface was left unsmoothed. The vertical handles rule out the possibility that they might have been produced on a rotating lathe.

WOODEN ARTIFACTS

Wooden artifacts are rare finds in the material culture of the ancient Near East, and few specimens from the Roman period have survived. Therefore, the considerable quantity of organic finds coming from the Judean Desert is an exceptional occurrence. Because of the unusually arid climatic conditions, many wooden objects—bowls, boxes, mirror frames, and combs—were retrieved. Their fine state of preservation facilitates the study of ancient woodworking techniques.

28
BOWL

52.40

First century B.C.E.
Height 4.9 cm (1¹⁵⁄₁₆ in.), diameter 26 cm (10¼ in.)

This deep bowl has a flat base, expertly turned on a lathe. Several concentric circles are incised on the base, and the rim of the bowl is rounded. Most of the wooden objects found in the Qumran area are of *acacia tortilis,* a tree prevalent in the southern wadis (valleys) of Israel.

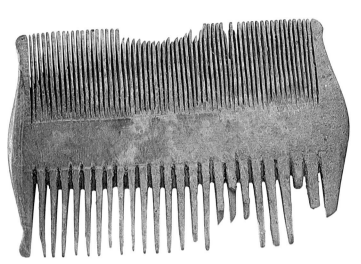
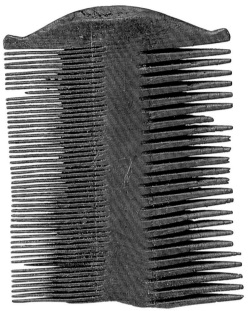

Similar to most of the ancient combs, these boxwood combs are two-sided. One side has closely spaced teeth for straightening the hair, and the opposite side provides more teeth—for delousing.

29
COMBS
Boxwood
52.3, 52.3a
*Comb A: Length 6 cm
(2⅜ in.), width 9.5 cm
(3¾ in.)*
*Comb B: Length 6.3 cm
(2½ in.), width 8 cm
(3⅛ in.)*

The Judean Desert has yielded a fair number of leather objects, permitting study of ancient tanning techniques. Water skins, large bags, pouches, purses, sandals, and garments have been found in the varied desert sites.

The majority of leather objects are of sheepskin. A few pieces, particularly those used as patches, are of goatskin and calfskin. The skins were vegetable tanned, mostly with gall and pomegranates. Most of the items shown date from the first century B.C.E. to the first century C.E.

Shown here are sandal soles of the *soleae* type. Intact sandals similar to these were found at Masada and in the Cave of Letters, all in the same region, although representing a range of several centuries.

These soles are made up of three layers of leather secured with leather bindings. Through slits situated near the heel, tabs entered the upper sole. The upper part of each tab was pierced by two vertical slits through which the main strap was threaded. The two ends of the main strap were then threaded into a slit on the upper part of the sandal, near the toe, where they were tied, holding the foot onto the sole.

30
SANDAL
Length 22 cm (8⅝ in.),
width 6.8 cm (2⅝ in.)

31
SANDAL
Length 21 cm (8¼ in.),
width 5.5 cm (2⅛ in.)

**LEATHER SCROLL
FASTENERS**

**32
TABS**
*Length 1.7–2.7 cm
(¹¹⁄₁₆–1¹⁄₁₆ in.), width
1.4–3.3 cm (⁹⁄₁₆–1⁵⁄₁₆ in.)*

**33
THONGS**
*Length 7–30 cm
(2³⁄₄–11³⁄₄ in.), width
0.3–0.8 cm (¹⁄₈–⁵⁄₁₆ in.)*

The tabs and thongs shown here were most likely used to bind and secure individual scrolls. The fastening is thought to consist of a slotted tab folded over the edge of the scroll (see catalog no. 2) with a thong inserted through its slot. The thong could be tightened and then wound around the scroll. The fasteners were generally made of leather and were prepared in different sizes. The leather thongs may have also been used in the making of phylacteries. (See the related diagram on page 135.)

Reference
Carswell, J. "Fastenings on the Qumrân Manuscripts." In *Qumrân Grotte 4: II. Discoveries in the Judaean Desert, VI*, pp. 23–28 and plates. Oxford, 1977.

34
PHYLACTERY CASES
Leather
4Q Phyl cases 1008
*Case A: Length 3.2 cm
(1¼ in.), width 1 cm
(⅜ in.)*
*Case B: Length 2.2 cm
(⅞ in.), width 1.2 cm
(½ in.)*
*Case C: Length 2 cm
(¾ in.), width 1 cm
(⅜ in.)*
*Case D: Length 2.3 cm
(⅞ in.), width 2.6 cm
(1 in.)*
*Case E: Length 1.3 cm
(½ in.), width 2.1 cm
(13⁄16 in.)*

Case A

This phylactery case has two parts, stitched together. It is a four-compartment type case, worn on the head. Each compartment held a minute roll of the type exhibited in catalog no. 3. Cases B, C, and D are similar to this four-compartment case.

Case E

Worn on the arm, this case has only one compartment. It is formed of a single piece of leather folded in two, with one half deeply stamped out to contain a minute roll. A fine leather thong was inserted at the middle, and the halves were folded over and stitched together.

Reference

Discoveries in the Judaean Desert, I, p. 7.

A

B

C

D

E

The textiles here are two out of scores of pieces collected together with scrolls and other objects from the floor of Qumran Cave 1 in the spring of 1949. The textiles were examined at the H. M. Norfolk Flax Establishment in England, and the material was identified as linen. A total of seventy-seven pieces, plain and decorated, were cataloged and described by the renowned textile expert Grace M. Crowfoot, on whose report the following description is based.

All of the pieces appear to have come from small cloths, definitely shaped and sewn. The full measurements of the cloths vary between 57 by 50 centimeters (the largest) and 27 by 23 centimeters (the smallest). They usually have one or two cut edges, hinting that the original loom-woven cloth was larger and wider. These edges were rolled and whipped with a single or double thread. The yarn used in the cloth is all S-spun (the direction of the fiber twist forming an S shape); two-ply thread was sometimes used for sewing. The spinning is fairly good, the warp usually harder and more even than the weft. The linen is generally of fair quality; the highest counts recorded are 18 by 18 and 20 by 16 threads per centimeter, while the lowest are 10 by 8 threads per centimeter. It seems, however, that the weavers were aiming at an even linen weave.

Several cloths have a corded starting border, such as catalog no. 35. It is formed by two groups of threads twined through the warp loops. The warp threads were crossed before the weave started. These details indicate the use of a somewhat primitive loom: possibly the warp-weighted loom, or the two-beamed vertical loom. The quality of both thread and cloth seems to indicate that the linen is a local product.

The only form of colored decoration, although rare, is blue lines, usually two, of indigo-dyed linen threads in the weft. The majority of the cloths are plain, however, some with simple or somewhat more elaborate fringe and with or without an open space. The practice of leaving an open space at one or both ends of a cloth is an ancient tradition and here may have served as a sole ornament: in antiquity decorative bands were usually made with dyed wool because of the extreme difficulty of dying linen; however, this is nonexistent here, probably as a result of the biblical prohibition of *sha'atnez*—the mixing of wool and linen.

It seems probable that all of the cloths from Qumran are linked in one way or another with the scrolls. Some of them were certainly scroll wrappers; the remains of one scroll was found wrapped in a small square of linen. Other cloths, found folded into pads, may have formed a packing for worn-out scrolls inside the jars. Still other pieces—with corners twisted or tied round with linen cord (catalog no. 36)—were probably protective covers, tied over the jar tops.

The materials used as scroll wrappers in the ancient world seem to have varied. The Mishnah, referring to wrappers for the scrolls of the Law, relates: "Handkerchiefs, wrappers for scrolls [of the Law] and bath towels do not come under the law of Diverse Kinds. But R. Eliezer forbids them [if they have in them wool and linen]" (Kil. 9.3). From this it may be inferred that they were usually of linen alone.

Scroll wrappers, when old and worn out, were destined to be deposited together with sacred books in a *genizah* (a storehouse for discarded Hebrew writings and ritual articles). When the *genizah* was too full, the contents were appropriately buried in the cemetery.

It seems reasonable that the majority of the cloths at Qumran were used as scroll wrappers. The wrapped scrolls may have been concealed in a cave at a time of national panic. The concealment also may have constituted the burial of the contents of a *genizah*. The condition of the cloths would coincide with either suggestion.

It is interesting to note that the textiles, of both wool and linen, found at the Murabba'at Cave and in the Cave of Letters, also in the Dead Sea area, are of much greater variety and are parts of garments—tunics, mantles, belts, and kerchiefs, as well as spreads, sacks, nets, and more.

Tamar Schick

Reference
Crowfoot, G. M. "The Linen Textiles." In *Qumran Cave 1*. Discoveries in the Judaean Desert, I, pp. 18–38. Oxford, 1955.

35
LINEN CLOTH
7Q, cloth 30
Length 35.5 cm (13⅞ in.),
width 24 cm (9⅜ in.)
Counts: 14 × 14, 13 × 13,
and in one place 16 × 14
threads per cm

This cloth has edges cut along three sides, rolled and oversewn with a single thread; the fourth edge is a corded starting border in twining technique, followed by a woven strip and an open unwoven space. It was found folded into a pad and was probably used as packing for discarded scrolls.

Reference
Discoveries in the Judaean Desert, I, pp. 33–34. Oxford, 1955.

The edges of this cloth are cut, rolled, and whipped on two opposite sides with single thread; on the other two, double thread was used. Two corners are twisted, and the third has a piece of string knotting it, indicating its probable use as a cover for a scroll jar.

Reference
Discoveries in the Judaean Desert, I, p. 31. Oxford, 1955.

36
LINEN CLOTH
1Q, cloth 15
Length 29 cm
(11 5/16 in.), width 25 cm
(9¾ in.)
Counts: 17 × 13 threads
per cm

BASKETRY

Basketry, together with cordage, represents a major type of perishable material retrieved in the arid part of Israel. The basketry fragments on display are made of date palm leaves, a material convenient for making baskets and mats. The technique used is a type of plaiting that was popular during Roman times and remained in favor through the following centuries; a variant is still used in the Near East today.

37
BASKET FRAGMENTS
Palm leaves
11Q
Fragment A:
Length 26 cm (10⅛ in.),
width 16.5 cm (6½ in.).
Three courses preserved
Fragment B:
Length 21.2 cm (8¼ in.),
width 19.5 cm (7⅝ in.).
Four courses preserved
Technique: Braid of 13
elements in 2/2 twill
plaiting

Because of the exceptional conditions inside caves in the Dead Sea region, several baskets and mats of plaited weave survived intact. Their survival permitted the reconstruction of the Qumran plaited basket, made of a single braid (*zefira* in Mishnaic terms) composed of several elements (*qala'ot*) and spiraling from base to rim. The coiled braid was not sewn together; instead, successive courses were joined around cords as the weaving progressed. In a complete basket the cords are not visible, but they form horizontal ridges and a ribbed texture. Each basket had two arched handles made of palm-fiber rope. Much ingenuity is displayed by the way in which they were attached to the rims: by passing reinforcing cords through the plaited body of the basket.

Basketware was probably very common, as it is to this day, in varied household activities. However, in times of need, baskets and mats also served for collecting and wrapping the bones and skulls of the dead.

Tamar Schick

A   B – D

CORDAGE

The cordage on display represents items of varying thickness and use. The raw materials include palm leaves, palm fibers, and rushes. Fragment A probably represents a ridge or reinforcing cord. B–D are heavier cords and might have been used in packing and tying bundles and water skins. Fragment E is a detached handle. The free-standing end of a handle cord that links the handle to the basket can be discerned in one of the loops.

E

APPENDIX

The Paleo-Hebrew and Jewish Scripts

Ada Yardeni

The ancient Hebrew script, also known as the paleo-Hebrew script, is one of the offshoots of the Phoenician script. It was the exclusive Hebrew script of the First Temple period from about 850 to 586 B.C.E., in both the Judean and the Israelite kingdoms.

In the wake of the destruction of the First Temple (586 B.C.E.) and the ensuing exile, Hebrew lost its prominent, singular status in favor of Aramaic, which had become the official language of the Persian empire. In the Post-Exilic period, in the Diaspora and in Judea as well, the cursive Aramaic script gradually replaced the ancient Hebrew script for secular writing as well as for holy scriptures. (Jewish tradition maintains that Ezra the Scribe established that custom on returning from the Babylonian exile.) The paleo-Hebrew script, however, was not completely abandoned. Although of limited use, it apparently held a high nationalistic and religious status and was used particularly in priestly circles, as well as in times of nationalistic strife or revival. The paleo-Hebrew script appears on a variety of materials: stone, pottery, coins, and papyrus. However, the major finds in this script from the late Second Temple period are from Qumran. Paleo-Hebrew characters are used for about a dozen biblical scrolls and, interestingly, are employed for writing the Tetragrammaton, the four-letter divine name (see catalog no. 5), and occasionally in manuscripts otherwise written in the Jewish script.

The major changes that occurred in the paleo-Hebrew script were the leveling of the height of the letters of the alphabet (the Jewish script underwent a similar process) and changes in the stance of the letters. Of chronological significance are the changes in the length of the downstrokes and in the inclination of the letters toward the ensuing letters. However, a proper cursive style did not evolve in paleo-Hebrew script, possibly because of its limited use.

Of special interest is the Leviticus Scroll from Qumran (catalog no. 4), written in the paleo-Hebrew script. The Leviticus fragments were dated on paleographical grounds (their script resembling the script on Hasmonean coins) to the late second–early first century B.C.E. The almost uniform direction of the downstrokes, sloping to the left, indicates an experienced, rapid, and rhythmic hand. A version of the paleo-Hebrew script is used today by the Samaritans.

The Jewish script is one of the offshoots of the late formal Aramaic cursive script. It emerged when the latter split into local scripts following the fall of the Persian empire in the second half of the fourth century B.C.E.

A group of dated documents, the latest from 335 B.C.E., found at Wadi Daliyeh along the Jordan Valley, is in the late Aramaic script. It bears affinity with the script of the earliest Qumran scroll fragments (4QSam[b]), which may be regarded as a link between the Aramaic and the Jewish scripts. Certain late Aramaic letter forms prevail in documents written in early Jewish script (such as the looped *alef* and the looped *tav*, the final *lamed*, and the final *nun*, etc.).

The earliest dated document in the Jewish script is from Wadi Murabba'at, dated to the second year of the emperor Nero (55/56 C.E.). Because no Qumran document yet published bears an explicit date, Qumran scholars must rely on historical, archeological, and paleographical data. Thus, the earliest documents from Qumran have been dated to the late third or early second century B.C.E. Formal development of the letters is reflected, for example, in the straightening of the curved strokes resulting in the formation of angular joins, which give the Jewish bookhand its square appearance. Another characteristic is the regularity of the writing, which is a result of the suspension of the letters on horizontal guidelines (not attested in Aramaic documents written in ink). At this early stage of independent development, the letters in the Jewish script were not yet adorned with ornamental additions, except for the inherited serifs in several letters (for example, *dalet, kaf, mem, qof,* and *resh*). The distinction between thick horizontal and thin vertical strokes, characteristic of the late Aramaic scripts, is still evidenced in the earliest documents from Qumran—and occasionally even in later documents—but is not typical of the Jewish script.

Three main periods in the development of the Jewish script are distinguished: the Hasmonean period (167–30 B.C.E.), the Herodian period (30 B.C.E.–70 C.E.), and the post-Herodian period (70–135 C.E.). The majority of Qumran documents belong to the first two periods, although some earlier fragments are available. The variety of handwritings testifies to the activity of scores of scribes. It is reasonable, therefore, to believe that a great many documents found in the caves of Qumran came from other places.

Fragments of the Book of Enoch (catalog no. 11) include fine examples of early Hasmonean script. The Prayer for King Jonathan (Alexander Jannaeus, 103–76 B.C.E.) (catalog no. 2), dated to the first quarter of the first century B.C.E., exhibits a variety of letter forms in bookhand as well as semicursive and cursive hands (for example, three forms of the letter *mem*).

A significant increase in ornamental elements in the letters—in the form of independent additional strokes—is evidenced in the Herodian period, together with the leveling of the height of the letters. Examples of the Herodian script here include the Psalms Scroll (catalog no. 5), the Hosea Commentary (no. 6), and the Songs of the Sabbath Sacrifice (no. 9). It also is characterized by the crystallization of different script styles, such as the calligraphic bookhand (later to develop into the ornamental script style used for Torah scrolls), and the standard cursive script style that prevailed in Judea during the late Herodian and the post-Herodian periods. It went out of use at the end of the Bar Kokhba revolt (135 C.E.). This cursive style served for official as well as literary documents: an early form appears, for example, in one of the manuscripts of Enoch from Qumran (4Q212), and its later forms are attested on ossuaries and inscriptions from the Herodian period, on ostraca from Masada dating to the end of the Herodian period, and in documents from the late first and early second centuries C.E. The Jewish bookhand continued to exist and developed many script styles in widely dispersed Jewish communities. The Hebrew script used today is its modern descendant.

	PALEO- HEBREW 8th century B.C.E.	JEWISH SCRIPT Temple Scroll	ORIENTAL* 9th–10th centuries	SEFARDI 13th–15th centuries	ASHKENAZI 14th–15th centuries
alef					
bet					
gimmel					
dalet					
he					
vav					
zayin					
ḥet					
tet					
yod					
kaf					
final kaf					
lamed					

STYLES OF HEBREW SCRIPT

PALEO-HEBREW	JEWISH SCRIPT	ORIENTAL*	SEFARDI	ASHKENAZI	
8th century B.C.E.	Temple Scroll	9th–10th centuries	13th–15th centuries	14th–15th centuries	
					mem
					final mem
					nun
					final nun
					samech
					ayin
					peh
					final peh (feh)
					ẓade
					final ẓade
					qof
					resh
					shin
					tav

* Includes handwritings used in the Near East and North Africa

Preservation of the Scroll Fragments

Esther Boyd-Alkalay

The arid and constant climatic conditions in the Judean Desert caves facilitated the survival of the scrolls and other organic materials found in the area. To preserve the fragile scroll fragments, the Israel Antiquities Authority established and developed a conservation laboratory at its premises in the Rockefeller Museum building in Jerusalem. The scroll fragments are housed in an environment that maintains constant relative humidity and temperature.

The writing material of the scrolls came chiefly from sheep and goat skins, which were prepared in a variety of methods. The appearance of the fragments ranges considerably in color and surface texture, as well as in state of preservation. The writing, in black, black-brown, and occasionally red ink, usually appears on only one side of the skin. Detailed research on the exact character of the skins, the inks, and the changes that could have occurred over the years is under way.

A general evaluation of the condition of the fragments and a review of earlier storage conditions are being supported by laboratory analysis and collegial consultation. The inexperience of the early scroll researchers in considering preservation requirements led to treatment that has proven over time to be inappropriate. Early efforts to hold together fragments involved the use of pressure-sensitive tapes (cellotape) that have since deteriorated, leaving sticky residues and stains. A major effort to remove the adhesives is in progress. These involve time-consuming and painstaking processes being carried out by a team of expert conservators who document and evaluate each fragment in detail to determine the required treatment.

The fragments, which had been sandwiched between sheets of glass or acidic cardboards, are being rehoused using archival-quality boards and hinges. The new housing system will permit future rearrangements and reconstruction.

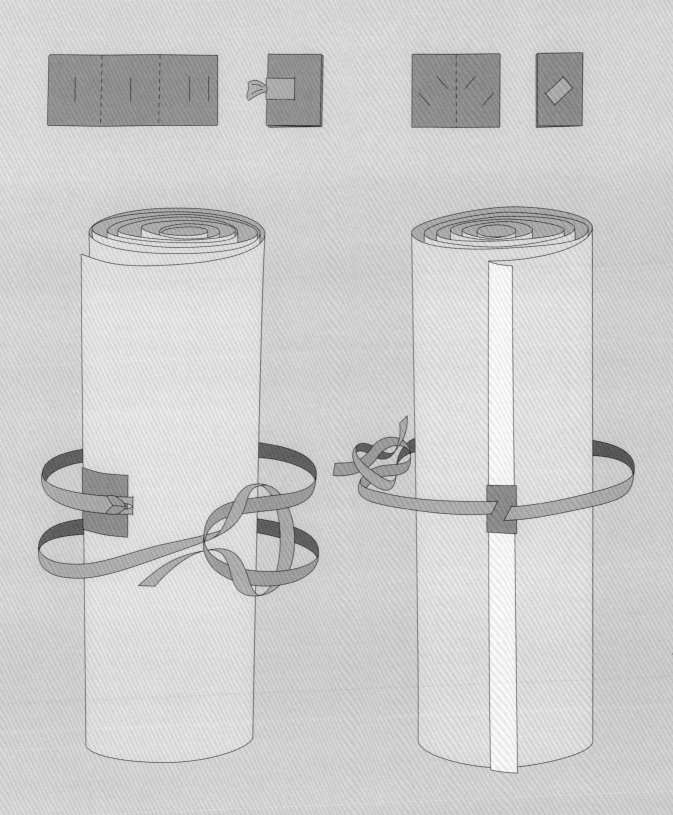

RECONSTRUCTION OF SCROLLS SHOWING
TWO TYPES OF FASTENINGS AND REINFORCING TABS

EPILOGUE: PUBLICATION OF THE DEAD SEA SCROLLS

Emanuel Tov

Tens of thousands of inscribed fragments of parchment—pieces from almost one thousand compositions, mainly literary documents—were found in the Judean Desert, particularly the Qumran area, beginning in 1947. The majority, fragments of some eight hundred documents, come from the caves around Qumran, while remnants of more than 150 documents and compositions were found in other locations in the Judean Desert—for example, Naḥal Ḥever, Wadi Murabbaʿat, Naḥal Ṣeʿelim, and Masada. Several compositions were preserved in large scrolls, while others are single-page documents.

Well-preserved texts included long ones such as the Isaiah Scroll from Cave 1 (twenty-four feet) and the Temple Scroll from Cave 11 (twenty-nine feet), but most of the compositions were fragmentary. The pieces were sorted into hundreds of groups, and, like working jigsaw puzzles, scholars attempted to assemble comprehensible texts. The tiny fragment of Chronicles (4Q118) represents all that has been preserved of the sixty-five biblical chapters of 1–2 Chronicles. But a more difficult and more representative case is that of the pseudo-Ezekiel literature, for which there are tens of fragments representing an unknown percentage of an unknown number of compositions.

The texts from the Judean Desert include more than 200 scrolls of biblical compositions, several hundred varied literary compositions, and a limited number of nonliterary documents. These documents, in Hebrew, Aramaic, Nabatean, and Greek, are of crucial importance for the study of the early exegesis of the Bible, its textual transmission, and the Hebrew and Aramaic languages, as well as the literature and the history of ideas of the Second Temple period.

Full publication of this complex corpus of documents has taken longer than was envisaged by the small team assigned in the 1950s to publish the newly found texts. Publication will include identification; decipherment; transcription; reconstruction; annotation on matters of paleography, text, and meaning; dating; and, in the case of the nonbiblical texts, translation as well. All of these elements, accompanied by facsimiles of the texts, are included in the official edition, published by the Oxford University Press, Discoveries in the Judaean Desert (DJD). Volumes one to nine have appeared to date, two volumes are now in press, and additional volumes are planned over the next seven years. A team of fifty-five scholars from nine countries—expanded from the original eight persons in the 1950s—is engaged in this project at present.

Apart from publication of the texts in the official DJD series, many texts have been published preliminarily (see E. Tov, "The Unpublished Qumran Texts from Caves 4 and 11," *Biblical Archaeologist* 55(2) (1992): 94–104).

Photographs of all of the texts from the Judean Desert are accessible to scholars. In 1993 they will be available on microfiche (E. J. Brill, Leiden).

OFFICIAL SERIES

Discoveries in the Judaean Desert. 9 vols. to date. Oxford: Clarendon Press, 1955–.

Vol. I: Barthélemy, D., and J. T. Milik. *Qumran Cave I*. 1955.

Vol. II: Benoit, P., J. T. Milik, and R. de Vaux. *Les Grottes de Murabba‘ât*. 1961.

Vol. III: Baillet, M., J. T. Milik, and R. de Vaux. *Les 'Petites Grottes' de Qumran*. 1962.

Vol. IV: Sanders, J. A. *The Psalms Scroll of Qumrân Cave 11 (11QPsᵃ)*. 1965.

Vol. V: Allegro, J. M. *Qumrân Cave 4: I (4Q158–4Q186)*. 1968.

Vol. VI: De Vaux, R., and J. T. Milik. *Qumrân Grotte 4: II (Archéologie et 4Q128–4Q157)*. 1977.

Vol. VII: Baillet, M. *Qumrân Grotte 4: III (4Q482–4Q520)*. 1982.

Vol. VIII: Tov, E. *The Greek Minor Prophets Scroll from Naḥal Ḥever (8ḤevXIIgr) (The Seiyâl Collection I)*. 1990.

Vol. IX: Skehan, P., E. Ulrich, and J. Sanderson, with a contribution by P. J. Parsons. *Qumran Cave 4: IV. Palaeo-Hebrew and Greek Biblical Manuscripts*. 1992.

TRANSCRIPTIONS, REPRODUCTIONS, AND RECONSTRUCTIONS

The Dead Sea Scrolls on Microfiche: A Comprehensive Facsimile Edition of the Texts from the Judaean Desert. Edited by E. Tov. Printed catalog by S. Reed. Israel Antiquities Authority. Leiden: E. J. Brill, forthcoming.

A Facsimile Edition of the Dead Sea Scrolls. Prepared with an introduction and index by R. Eisenman and J. Robinson. 2 vols. Washington, D.C.: Biblical Archaeology Society, 1991.

A Preliminary Edition of the Unpublished Dead Sea Scrolls: The Hebrew and Aramaic Texts from Cave Four. Reconstructed and edited by B. Wacholder and M. Abegg. 2 fascs. Washington, D.C.: Biblical Archaeology Society, 1991–92.

The Scroll of the War of the Sons of Light Against the Sons of Darkness. Edited by Y. Yadin. Translated by B. and C. Rabin. Oxford: Oxford University Press, 1962.

Scrolls from Qumrân Cave I: The Great Isaiah Scroll, the Order of the Community, the Pesher to Habakkuk. Photographs by J. Trever. Jerusalem: Albright Institute of Archaeological Research and the Shrine of the Book, 1972.

The Temple Scroll. Edited by Y. Yadin. 3 vols. Jerusalem: Israel Exploration Society, 1977–83.

GENERAL SOURCES

Baumgarten, J. *Studies in Qumran Law*. Studies in Judaism in Late Antiquity, vol. 24. Leiden: E. J. Brill, 1977.

Cross, F. *The Ancient Library of Qumran and Modern Biblical Studies*. The Haskell Lectures, 1956–57. Garden City, N.Y.: Doubleday, 1958.

————. "The Development of the Jewish Scripts." In *The Bible and the Ancient Near East: Essays in Honor of William Foxwell Albright*. Edited by G. Wright. Garden City, N.Y.: Doubleday, 1961.

SELECTED
READINGS

The Damascus Document Reconsidered. Edited by M. Broshi. Jerusalem: Israel Exploration Society and Shrine of the Book, 1992.

The Dead Sea Scrolls: Forty Years of Research. Edited by D. Dimant and U. Rappaport. Leiden: E. J. Brill, 1992.

De Vaux, R. *Archaeology and the Dead Sea Scrolls.* Oxford: Oxford University Press, 1973.

Fitzmyer, J. *The Dead Sea Scrolls: Major Publications and Tools for Study.* Society of Biblical Literature Resources for Biblical Study, no. 20. Atlanta: Scholars Press, 1990.

——————. *Responses to 101 Questions on the Dead Sea Scrolls.* New York: Paulist Press, 1992.

Flusser, D. *Judaism and the Origins of Christianity.* Jerusalem: Magnes Press, 1988.

Golb, N. "The Dead Sea Scrolls: A New Perspective." *The American Scholar* 58 (Spring 1989): 177–207.

Qumran and the History of the Biblical Text. Edited by F. Cross and S. Talmon. Cambridge: Harvard University Press, 1975.

Schechter, S. *Documents of Jewish Sectaries.* 1910. Reprint. Library of Biblical Studies. New York: KTAV Publishing House, 1970.

Schiffman, L. *The Halakhah at Qumran.* Studies in Judaism in Late Antiquity, vol. 16. Leiden: E. J. Brill, 1975.

Talmon, S. *The World of Qumran from Within: Collected Studies.* Jerusalem: Magnes Press; Leiden: E. J. Brill, 1989.

Tov, E. "The Unpublished Qumran Texts from Caves 4 and 11." *Journal of Jewish Studies* 43 (Spring 1992): 101–36.

Understanding the Dead Sea Scrolls: A Reader from the Biblical Archaeology Review. Edited by H. Shanks. New York: Random House, 1992.

Vermes, G. *The Dead Sea Scrolls: Qumran in Perspective.* Rev. ed. Philadelphia: Fortress Press, 1977.

——————. *The Dead Sea Scrolls in English.* 3rd ed. London: Penguin, 1990.

Wieder, N. *The Judean Scrolls and Karaism.* London: East and West Library, 1962.

Wilson, E. *Israel and the Dead Sea Scrolls.* New York: Farrar, Straus and Giroux, 1978.

Yadin, Y. *The Temple Scroll: The Hidden Law of the Dead Sea Sect.* New York: Random House, 1985.

Michael W. Grunberger

For this exhibition and catalog, kind advice was extended to us by a number of colleagues, all specialists in their fields. We are particularly indebted to Professors J. Greenfield and E. Tov of the Hebrew University; M. Broshi of the Shrine of the Book; Professor E. Qimron of Ben Gurion University at Beersheba; and R. Cohen, deputy director of the Israel Antiquities Authority, for reading our manuscript or parts thereof and offering information and advice.

We would like to extend our thanks to our colleagues at the Israel Antiquities Authority, without whom this exhibition would not have been possible: Jacob Fisch, who coordinated the logistics of the exhibit; Sarah Ben Arieh, Esther Boyd-Alkalay, and Tamar Schick; and Lena Liebman, Tanya Bitter, and Olga Navitzky, whose treatment of the scrolls and steps taken toward their preservation allowed the exhibition.

The studio photographs are chiefly the work of Yoram Lehman, Tsila Sagiv, and Clara Amit. Area photographs are by Duby Tal and David Harris.

We thank them all for their efforts.

Ayala Sussmann and Ruth Peled, Israel Antiquities Authority

ACKNOWL-EDGMENTS

It was clear from the inception of the exhibition that to complete it in the time allotted we would need the generous and timely assistance of a multitude of experts in Israel and the United States. First and foremost we are grateful to Amir Drori, director of the Israel Antiquities Authority, whose idea it was to mount a traveling exhibition featuring these scrolls. His aspiration could not have been realized without the steadfast support of Librarian of Congress James H. Billington, whose keen interest in the project ensured its successful completion.

At the Library of Congress, Irene Burnham, director of the interpretive programs office, provided overall direction for this exhibition, including its national program. Doris A. Hamburg, acting conservation officer, developed the conservation specifications for the exhibition objects, designed the housings used to mount the scrolls, oversaw the shipping and packing of the objects at each venue, and prepared the interim and final condition reports. Annlinn Krug Grossmann, conservator, fabricated all the scroll housings, and Margaret R. Brown, senior conservator, compiled the condition notebooks and provided additional conservation support. Tambra Johnson, registrar, planned and implemented the complex set of travel arrangements for couriers and cargo from Jerusalem to Washington, New York, and San Francisco and back to Jerusalem and prepared the various applications required to organize an international traveling exhibition. Norma Baker, director of the development office, served as liaison with the exhibition's sponsors and venues. John Kominski, general counsel, was instrumental in formulating the various agreements that support this international loan exhibition.

We are pleased to acknowledge the assistance of colleagues in Israel and the United States who have made this complicated undertaking possible. At the Israel Antiquities Authority we thank Jacob Fisch, director of marketing; Ruth Peled, chief curator; Tamar Schick, curator of organic materials; and Ayala Sussmann, director of publications. At the New York Public Library we are grateful for the cooperation of Leonard S. Gold, Dorot chief librarian of the Jewish Division; Susan F. Saidenberg, manager of exhibitions; Jean Mihich, registrar; Lou Storey, exhibitions designer and installation specialist; and Bonnie Rosenblum, manager of corporate relations. At the Fine Arts Museums of San Francisco we thank Melissa Leventon, acting curator of textiles, and Harry S. Parker III, director, for their participation and helpful suggestions.

Dana Pratt, director of the publishing office, played a key role in enabling this catalog to be published. We are indebted to Diane Maddex, president of Archetype Press, who oversaw and coordinated all aspects of this publication, and Robert L. Wiser, art director, who was responsible for its design.

We are deeply grateful to Mark E. Talisman, president of Project Judaica Foundation, whose early and continuing support for this exhibition enabled the participants to begin the critical planning and conservation tasks that permitted it to traverse the gulf between dream and reality—in record time.

Michael W. Grunberger, Library of Congress

CONTRIBUTORS

Donald T. Ariel is curator of numismatics, Israel Antiquities Authority.

Esther Boyd-Alkalay is restoration consultant, Israel Antiquities Authority.

Michael W. Grunberger is head of the Hebraic Section, Library of Congress.

Ruth Peled is chief curator, Israel Antiquities Authority, and co-curator of Scrolls from the Dead Sea.

Tamar Schick is curator of organic materials, Israel Antiquities Authority.

Ayala Sussmann is director of publications, Israel Antiquities Authority, and co-curator of Scrolls from the Dead Sea.

Emanuel Tov is professor of biblical literature, Hebrew University of Jerusalem, and editor-in-chief of the Dead Sea Scrolls Publication Project, Israel Antiquities Authority.

Ada Yardeni is research fellow in paleography, Hebrew University of Jerusalem.

Unless otherwise indicated, photographs in this catalog have been used with permission of the Israel Antiquities Authority.

Page 1: Scroll fragment featuring commentary *(pesher)* on the biblical verses of Hosea 2:8–14 (catalog no. 6; see pages 56–59). (Israel Antiquities Authority)

Page 19: A conservator with the Israel Antiquities Authority working on one of the scroll fragments. (Israel Antiquities Authority)

Page 34: Qumran and the Dead Sea seen from a scroll cave. (David Harris, Jerusalem)

Page 84: Aerial view of the Qumran ruin. (Duby Tal, Albatross Studio, Tel Aviv)

Pages 132–33: Chart adapted from "Styles of Hebrew Scripts," *Scribes, Script and Books* by Leila Avrin, pp. 126–27 (Chicago, 1991). Used with permission of the American Library Association.

Page 141: Scroll diagram adapted from "Fastenings on the Qumrân Manuscripts," *Qumrân Grotte 4: II,* Discoveries in the Judaean Desert, VI, pp. 26–27 (Oxford, 1977). Used with permission of Clarendon Press and the Israel Antiquities Authority.

The translations on pages 45 and 49 are adapted from *Tanakh: A New Translation of the Holy Scriptures According to the Traditional Hebrew Text,* pp. 103–4 and 192 (Philadelphia, 1985). Used with permission of the Jewish Publication Society.

ILLUSTRATIONS AND CREDITS